Vaiyākaraṇabhūṣaṇa
of
Kauṇḍabhaṭṭa

(Lakārārtha-nirṇaya)

Volume II

Sri Garib Dass Oriental Series No. 244

Vaiyākaraṇabhūṣaṇa of Kauṇḍabhaṭṭa

(Lakārārtha-nirṇaya)

Volume II

English Translation

by

V.N. Jha

Sri Satguru Publications

A Division of

Indian Books Centre

Delhi - India

Published by :
Sri Satguru Publications
A Division of :
Indian Books Centre
Indological and Oriental Publishers
40/5, Shakti Nagar,
Delhi-110007
(INDIA)
Email : ibcindia@ibcindia.com

ISBN 81-7030-583-7

First Edition : Delhi, 1998

Published by Sunil Gupta for Sri Satguru Publications a division of Indian Books Centre, 40/5, Shakti Nagar, Delhi-110 007, India and printed at Mudran Bharti, Delhi-110007

Dedicated to

The sacred memory of
my revered teacher
Pandit T.S. Srinivasa Sastri

Acknowledgements

The students and colleagues of my Centre have helped me a lot in correcting the proofs of this volume. I am thankful to all of them.

I would also like to thank Indian Books Centre for their continued interest in bringing out scholarly works.

V.N. Jha

Director,

Centre of Advanced Study in Sanskrit,

University of Pune,

Pune - 411007

Preface

As mentioned in the first volume which contained the English Translation of the *Dhātvarthanirṇaya* - section of the *Vaiyākaraṇabhūṣaṇa* of Kauṇḍabhaṭṭa (or Koṇḍabhaṭṭa) I am presenting the English Translation of the second section of the same text, called *Lakārārtha-nirṇaya.* Since the original Sanskrit is in the style of a *vāda* - text, the free rendering in English is made in a dialogue form. I hope, the translation is readable and helpful in grouping the arguments of the Vaiyākaraṇas along with those of their opponents.

As mentioned in the preface of the first volume, this work is a highly mature contribution of Kauṇḍabhaṭṭa on the philosophy of Language. The *Vaiyākaraṇabhūṣaṇa* is a huge work and it contains thirteen sections on thirteen topics each one representing a particular part of Sanskrit expression. They are:

1. *Dhātvarthanirṇaya* (Discussion on the meaning of a verbal root)
2. *Lakārārtha-nirṇaya* (Discussion on the meaning of a personal suffix)
3. *Subarthanirṇaya* (Discussion on the meaning of a case-termination)
4. *Nāmārthanirṇaya* (Discussion on the meaning of a nominal bare)
5. *Samāsārthanirṇaya* (Discussion on the meaning of a compound form)
6. *Nañarthanirṇaya* (Discussion on the meaning of a negative particle)
7. *Nipātārtha-nirṇaya* (Discussion on the meaning of indiclinables)

8. *Bhāvapratyayārtha nirṇaya* (Discussion on the meaning of an abstract suffix)
9. *Devatāpratyayārthanirṇaya* (Discussion on the meaning of a deity-marker suffix)
10. *Abhedaikasaṁkhyānirṇaya* (Discussion on the meaning of *abhedaikatva*)
11. *Saṁkhyāvivakṣānirṇaya* (Discussion on the intension of a number)
12. *Ktvāpratyādīnām arthanirṇaya* (Discussion on the meaning of *–tvā* etc.)
13. *Sphoṭanirṇaya* (Discussion on the theory of *sphoṭa*)

With this volume we are completing two sections. The remaining eleven sections will be presented in sequence as and when they are ready.

I would like to put on record my sense of appreciation for Indian Books Centre for their keen and sustained interest in this scientific work.

Delhi **V.N. Jha**

14-01-1998

Lakārārthanirṇaya of Kauṇḍabhaṭṭa

(As in the earlier chapter the meaning of a root is discussed and determined) similarly (in the following two verses) the author is going to determine the meaning of each of the ten *lakāras*.

The *lakāras* such as *laṭ* etc. (i.e., five let *lakāras*) are to be understood (i.e. to be employed) in the senses of present, past,[1] unseen, remote, something happening to-morrow onwards, future, injunction etc., and request etc., respectively.[(In other words, *laṭ* is to be employed in the sense of present cf. *vartamāne laṭ* P.3.2.123), *liṭ* in the sense of past [1] (cf. *Parokṣe liṭ* p. 3.2.115), *luṭ* in the sense of happening tomorrow onwards (cf. *anadyatane luṭ* p.3.3.15) *lṛṭ* in the sense of future (cf. *lṛt śeṣe ca* p 3.3.12), *leṭ* in the sense of inducement, etc. (cf. Tiṅarthe leṭ p.3.4.7) and loṭ in the sense request etc. (cf. *vidhinimantraṇāmantraṇādhīṣṭasampraśna-prārthaneṣu liṅ* p. 3.3.161, *loṭ ca* p. 3.3.162, and *āśiṣi liṅloṭau* 3.3.173).

That *laṭ* has the sense of present is understood from the Paṇinian rule *vartamāne laṭ* (3.2.123.). *Vartamānatva* (characteristics of present tense) means that which is indicated by the action already begun but not yet finished; or being different from the past as well as the future, as is already popularly known *vartamānatva* is found in the action (*vyāpāra*) such as those beginning with the action of putting the cooking pot with rice and water on the fire-place till the pot is brought down the fire-place and therefore, with reference to that *laṭ* is employed.

Now, is this time (such as present) the indicated or expressed meaning of *laṭ* ? The first is not true (i.e. it is not indicate by iṭ) because that (present time) is not the meaning of the root. (After all what is the meaning of *dyotakatva* (being indicative)? *Dyotakatva* means being indicative of the significative power of the word by its side.[1] But it (*dyotakatva*) is not possible if the root has no significative power with regard to the time (present etc.)

It cannot be argued that roots have significative power with regard to the time (present etc.) since there are numerous roots and we will have to postulate numerous such powers and thus there will be the contingency of cumbrousness. On the other hand, since *laṭ* is only one in number it is but proper to assume that present tense is the expressed meaning of *laṭ*. Moreover, although there is a specific rule such as *vartamāne laṭ* (P 3.2.123) which enjoins *laṭ* in the sense of present tense still if *laṭ* is not taken as expressive of present tense it cannot be expressive of agent also. And it will be only indicative of the agent since there is no reason to take *kartā* (agent) as *vācya* whereas *vartamānatva* as *dyotya*. Therefore, the argument that let the root mean 'present tense' by *lakṣanā* (secondary signification) and let the *laṭ* be indicative of present tense and *dyotakatva* is nothing but the nature of what indicates the intention of the speaker is hereby refuted.

The second (i.e. 'present tense' is the expressed meaning of *laṭ*) is also not true because when *laṭ* has been satisfied by the meaning of *lakāra* assigned in a general way by the rule *laḥ karmaṇi ca bhāve cākarmakebhyaḥ* (P. 3.4.69) there is no scope for this (i.e. *vartamāne laṭ*) to assign the meaning 'present tense to it) Inspite of that if one thinks that P.3.2.123 operates in that case P.3.2.123 which is a special rule will set aside p.3.4.69 which is a general rule as per the maxim known as *takrakauṇḍinyanyāya*[3] and therefore agent cannot be the expressed meaning of *laṭ*.

What you have argued so far is not true because both the views (i.e. (i) present tense is indicated by *laṭ* and (2) it is expressed by laṭ) are expressed in the *Ākara grantha* and because both are established by reasoning. Thus, the present tense is indicated by *laṭ* because present tense is the meaning of the root and since that cannot be understood without *laṭ* it is but proper to say that *laṭ* indicates present tense. It cannot also be argued that if present tense is taken as the meaning of a root there will arise the contingency of the above mentioned fault (i.e., cumbarousness), because no extra-time other than the continuous activities is accepted and because their being the meaning of a root has already been established. Thus, time is nothing more than the actions themselves since there is no proof or authority to establish it as a separate entity. If, however, it is postulated that time is different from the activities, then one has to postulate the significative power (in the roots) and thus there would arise the contingency of cumbrousness. Moreover, if it is accepted that extra-time is the meaning, then it will go against the statement of the *Mahābhāṣya* which questions the correctness of the use of *laṭ* etc. in sentences such as *parvatās tiṣṭhanti* (mountains exist), *ātmāsti* (the self exists) etc.[4]

In fact, if *Patañjali* would have intended extra-time as *vartamāna* it was possible for him to endorse the correctness of *laṭ* in the above sentences such as *ātmāsti* etc. taking into account the action of the Sun etc. belonging to that time (of existence of mountain etc.) because that could have been easily got.

Similarly, it will go against the *siddhāntabhāṣya* which endorses the above usages by taking the action delimited by the action of the kings belonging to that time. When the actions of the sun etc. are easily available it is not proper to go that far.

In our opinion, however, since the action favorable to the existence of self has no beginning, the objection raised by *Patañjali* is quite proper because the definition of *vartamāna* such as 'that which has begun but not yet finished' does not apply in *ātmāsti* etc. Similarly, *Patañjali*'s answer on the basis of the beginning of the qualified action such as the action favorable to the existence of the self which is qualified or delimited by the action of the kings of that time is also quite apt.[5]

Kaiyaṭa also explains the *siddhāntabhāṣya* the same way. Taking the *pratīka* such as *iha bhūtabhaviṣyadāvartamānānāṁ rājñām yāḥ kriyās tās tiṣṭhater adhikaraṇam* (here the actions of the past, future, and present kings are the substratum of the existence (of the mountains) he explains that the different existence of the kings with reference to the time such as past etc. make the existence (i.e. *kriyārupatva* of mountain etc. different and hence the time is of the nature of action) and *kālatrayayoga* i.e. that the existence of mountain etc. can be related to all the three times (past etc.,) are befitting. Therefore, the explanation of the bhāṣya is based on the qualified difference (i.e., on the action qualified by other action). It is said in the *Vākyapadīya* that

Everything is differentiated by other thing; by itself nothing could be differentiated. Therefore, the existence of the mountain etc. is differentiated by the form of others (i.e. by the actions of past, future and present kings). That the difference is caused by the difference of the qualified is clear from the explanation of the above verse in the commentary called *Helārājīya.* For the same reason it is stated in the *Śabdakaustubha* that the propriety of (the use of past tense) in the sentence *eko ha vai nārayaṇa āsīt* (The god *Nārāyaṇa* was alone) etc. can be justified only on the basis of *viśiṣṭabheda.*

Therefore, present tense is of the nature of action only. And it is but apt to take *Vartamānatva* residing in action as the indicated sense of *laṭ* which can be established through *anvaya* and *vyatireka*[6]. Similarly, not-coming-into-existence of the action is the meaning of future tense and conclusion of the action is the meaning of the past tense. Therefore, *laṭ* etc.[7] are to be employed in the respective sentences when that action is to be indicated as present and the like. Thus, *laṭ* is the indicator of present tense and this is the established tradition i.e., trodden path.

Similarly, there is no defect in accepting *vācakatva* of *laṭ* etc. Thus, present tense is the meaning of *laṭ* since that is the appropriate meaning of the rule *vatamāne laṭ* and because time is defined as the delimitor of action by *Vākyapadiya* saying 'time differentiates action alone, whereas number differentiates everything'. Nor is it reasonable to say that a thing is its own delimitor. Moreover, since action can be known (by the root) even without *laṭ*, the *vartamānatva* residing in that (action) alone is to be accepted as indicated (by *laṭ*). In that case, that (*vartamānatva*) also is to be taken as the *śakyārtha* of the root and as such it will entitle postulating many significative powers for many roots. Instead of that it is better to postulate significative power with reference to *vartamānatva* for only one *laṭ* on the strength of economy. Moreover, you should say that association of *laṭ with the root* is the cause for the knowledge of action qualified by *vartamānatva*. In that case, since the position remains the same[8] let the *laṭ* be exclusively expressive of *vartamānatva*. If it is accepted *as such*, then *kartā* cannot be the meaning of *laṭ* because the special rule will set aside the general rule. It is not true because when both the meanings (such as 'agent' and 'present tense') are possible there is no question of one rule being *bādhya* and another being *bādhaka*[9] That is why it is said– 'if both can be these, *there* is possibility or scope'. Moreover, in that case[10] the rule *laḥ karmaṇi* (p.3.4.69) will have no scope (for its operation). In other place (such as *let* etc. also (it will have no scope for its operation) because it will be set aside or obstructed by the meanings injunction etc. In that case, as per the maxim "the rules affected by purposelessness or absence of scope act reversely with reference to strength or weakness (i.e. they become more powerful) the general rule will operate.

What you said that if time is taken as additional entity different from action it will go against the Bhāṣya quoted above (by us) is not true because that *was said* adopting the view-point that *laṭ* is the *dyotaka* (indicator) of present tense.

Actually speaking, even if time is taken as an additional entity the definition of *vartamānatva* remains the same i.e., that which is indicated by the action already begun but not yet finished. That definition, however, is not applicable in the case of *ātmāsti* etc. since the action (of the self) has no beginning and therefore, how is the *vartamānatva* possible was the import of the objection. And although the action (of the self) has no beginning in itself but when it is qualified by some other action it can be said that it has a beginning and therefore, since inductiveness of action is possible the definition of *Vartamānatva* etc. applies (in the case of *ātmāsti* etc.) This was the import of the *Siddāntabhāṣya*; it is to be understood.

As a matter of fact, time is not an extra entity but the action itself. The meaning of *laṭ* etc. is, however the *vartamānatva* etc., which is of the nature of 'being begun but not yet finished' etc. and which is existent in that action. It is what is meant ultimately. Therefore, *vartamānatva* is the expressed sense of *laṭ*.

In this way, in the case of *ātmāsti* (the self exists), *parvatās tiṣthanti* (the mountains exit) etc., *vartamānatva* befits and in the case of *atma āsīt* (there was darkness), (*tucchenābhyapihitaṁ yadāsīt*) *eko ha vai nārāyaṇa āsīt* (*Nārāyaṇa* alone was there) etc. *bhūtatva* (the nature of being past tense) also befits.

The meaning of *liṭ* is being described by *prarokṣe* etc. on the basis of the rule of *prarokṣe liṭ*. Time is, however, of two kinds: one belonging to to-day and the other belonging to other than 'today'. These two types (of time) can again be of the nature of past and future[11]. *Liṭ* is, however, enjoined in the sense of *anadyatana* remote past. This is the meaning of the *sūtra: prarokṣe liṭ*. Thus, *liṭ* is not used in the sense *adyatane* past, *anadyatane* future and past which is not remote. *Parokṣatva* (the nature of remote past) means not being the object of the knowledge which is possessed of the *viṣayatā* such as 'I perceive' and which is existent in the speaker.

Well (we feel that) the adjective *parokṣa* does not distinguish any action from the *aparokṣa* one because all actions are invariably imperceptible. It is also stated in the *Mahābhāṣya* that this one which is known as action is not at all seen and has its components existent in a particular sequence and hence cannot be shown collectively together as a mass.

Some say that it is not an insurmountable difficulty because what is intended here is the imperceptibility of the *kārakas* possessed of the power and favorable to the action as engaged in activities. So, even if mere *kārakas* not engaged in activities are seen, *liṭ* is used. For example, *ayaṁ papāca* (This person had cooked)[12] etc. Similarly, when one did not take notice of one's own activity, why it was being done due to absent-mindedness and later when that (activity) is inferred by the result, *liṭ* is undoubtedly used. For example, *bahu jagada purastāt tasya mattā kilāham* (I was mad indeed that I spoke so much before him (my husband)

However, *vyātene kiraṇāvalīm udayanaḥ*[13] (Udayana elaborately composed the (commentary called *Kiraṇāvalī*) is incorrect [14], Because although *parokṣatva* (the nature of being imperceptible) can be established somehow in the above-mentioned manner [15] still since *anadyatanatva* (the nature of being 'not of today' i.e. remoteness) and *atītatva* (nature of being past) cannot apply to the action of writing extensive work which consists of the composition of words that produce definite knowledge and which proclaims knowledge of the *Śāstra*, which can be achieved by much more concentration of mind. For this reason, the use of *liṭ* (in *vyātene kiraṇāvalīm udayanaḥ*) is grammatically incorrect.

But this is to be noted that *liṭ* is used when the action itself is imperceptible because it is in simple meaning of the *sūtra*: *parokṣe liṭ*

To get the *kārakas* of the action through the indicative power of the root.

Literally, the sūtra means " when *Dhātu* is *parokṣa liṭ* is added to it. This is absurd, since *Dhātu* cannot be *parokṣa*. Therefore it should mean by secondary signification the meaning of *Dhātu*. Then the relation between the word *Dhātu* and the action is *svavācyatva* i.e., the action is the expressed meaning of the root and so it is simple. If on the other hand we have (*gaurava* (cumbrousness) because from the *adhikāra*: *dhātoḥ* (P.3.1.91) (*dhātoḥ*) comes in the sūtra: *parokṣe liṭ* and since its primary meaning does not fit in the *sūtra*. the secondary meaning such as the meaning of the root (is adopted) by *lakṣaṇā* suggestive power) and in that case the relation between the meaning and the word expressive of that) is *svavācyatva* the nature of being the meaning of its own (here, of the root). (But if *parokṣa* is connected with *kārakas* engaged in action one has to adopt) *lakṣanā* in the relation between *dhātū* and its implication) and in that case the relation will be *svavācyasādhanatva* i.e. being the *kārakas* of the action which is the expressed sense of the root i.e. the nature of being a *kāraka* expressed by it (*dhātu*); (Thus, the cumbrousness).

The objection that one action cannot be distinguished from the other since all the actions are imperceptible is also not true because although the collection of actions is imperceptible each (of the collection) is not imperceptible. That is why, it is stated in the *Bhāṣya* that '(the action cannot be shown *collectively in a mass*).

For the same reason in the sentence *paśya mṛgo dhāvati* (look the deer is running) that the object of the verb *paśya* is the action of running (of the deer) is a fact unanimously accepted by all.

Nor can it be argued that each (of the collection of actions) is not action because even that (action) is the meaning of the root.

Even the *parokṣatva* described in the *Mahābhāṣya* fits to the action. This is the way (to solve the problems of this type).

The meaning of *luṭ* is stated by *śvo bhāvinyarthe* (in the sense of some action taking place tomorrow which means ' a future (action) not belonging to today', as per the *sūtra anadyatane luṭ* (P.3.3.15.); For example, in the sentence *śvo bhavitā* (some action) will take place tomorrow) etc.

The meaning of *lṛṭ* is stated by *bhavisyati* (in the sense of future) which means (*lṛṭ*) is used in the sense of future in general as per the *sūtra*: *lṛṭ śeṣe ca* (P.3.3.12); for example, in the sentence *ghato bhaviṣyatị* (a pot will come into existence) etc. The nature of being future tense means the nature of being possessed of 'coming into existence' or ' taking place' at a time which is a *pratiyogin* (counter-correlative) of antecedent non-existence belonging to present time.

The author states the meaning of *leṭ* by *vidhyādau* (in the sense of inducement etc.). On the basis of the rule *liṅarthe leṭ* (P.3.4.7) The word *ādi* (in *vidhyādau*) includes *nimantraṇa*, *āmantraṇa* , *adhīṣṭa* etc. *vidhi* means inducement. In other words it means directing the subordinates such as servants etc. *Nimantraṇa* means injunction i.e. employing or ordering daughter's son etc. in the obligaroty *śrāddhabhojana* (taking meals in the *śrāddha* ceremony). *Āmantraṇa* means permission to act as one desires. *Adhīṣṭa* means the act of requesting (someone) with respect. The sum and substance of the whole narration is that *liṅ* is used in the sense of injunction. Stating respectively all the four (*vidhi* etc.) is for the sake of explanation.

It is, therefore, said that 'the common feature of *pravartanā* (injunction) exists in all the four (varieties of injunction such as *vidhi* etc. and therefore, *liṅ* should have been enjoined in the sense of *pravartanā* only[16]. What is the purpose of stating its variety? (It may be replied that) stating the first four such as (*vidhi* etc) in the *sūṭra* 3.3.161., may be for the sake of explaining the *nyāya* (the variety of *pravartanā* and the occasion of its use) or for the sake of mere statement'.

For the same reason in the *siddhāntakaumudī* also it is stated (in the same way as it is stated above)[17].

There, *pravartanā* means some quality which is favorable to taking of efforts (or which causes (a man to act) i.e. being a means of (obtaining one's) desired (object), since *iṣṭasādhanatājñāna* (the knowledge of being a means of obtaining a desired result) is established as the cause for taking efforts in general it is but proper to take that (*iṣṭasādhanatva*) as the meaning (of *liṅ*)

Similar is the purport of the *sūtra* of *Jaimini* which runs as *śāstraphalaṁ prayoktari tallakṣaṇatvāt*[18]. (It means) the result such as heaven etc. mentioned in an injunctive sentence (goes to) the *prayoktṛ* i.e. the performer (of the sacrifice) because *vidhi* is of the nature of being the means to obtain the result of the doer. (Similarly) in the commentary on the *Brahmasūtra bhāṣya* called *Bhāmatī* under the section beginning with the *sūtra*: *kartā śāstrārthatvāt*[19], *vidhi* is explained as being the means to obtain the desired result of the agent.

Therefore, *Maṇḍana Miśra* [20] has said.:

'There is no other inducer of a man in actions except the property of being the means to obtain his desired result. Scholars call that property which is the cause for taking efforts as *pravartanā*.

Now, if you argue that as *iṣṭasādạnatva* (being the means to obtain the desired result) is the inducer (of a man to an action) similarly, *kṛtisādhyatva* (the state of being to be accomplished by action) is also the inducer and therefore, it (*kṛtisādhyatva*) can also be the expressed meaning of *liṅ*. An answer to this question is given in the first *pāda* of the first *adhyāya* in the *Anuvyākhyāna* (on the *Brahmasūtra*), as follows:

There is no such property as *kāryatā* (being fit to be done other than the nature of the means of the desired result. Nor is that a *kārya* which is invariably pervaded i.e., producible by an action because a prohibited act is also a thing that can be produced (but it should not be done). Nor can a future action be *kārya* since, in the sentence 'the god will create' there is nothing known as a *kārya*. Nor, that which cannot but be done, can be taken as *kārya* because in that case even a prohibited act may be a *kārya* (but it is not so). Therefore, both *iṣṭa* (desired one) and *sādhana* (the means to obtain that desired one) are the *kārya*.

It is explained in the *Nyāyasudhā* [21] in the following manner:

How is it that the *vedānta* works teach the pure *Brahman* [22], when it is a fact that a sentence results in being the informer (of something) associated with action and when it is also a fact that the understanding of the word-sense relationship is possible from the use of elderly persons only in association with action.

In order to remove this doubt that (*kāryatā* 'the nature of to-be-done') is being determined by '*kāryatā ca* etc. (in the first line of the above-mentioned *kārikās*) the words '*iṣṭatvam ca vinā* is to be added to the existing words *iṣṭasādhanatvām vinā* because in the last line it is stated so such as *tadiṣṭa-sādhanaṃ tathā*.

Kāryam etc. *vyāpya* means to be produced. Since the prohibited acts such as the killing of *brāhmins*, etc. are produced by actions, they the prohibited acts, too become *kārya* and therefore, it (i.e. which is produced by an action) is not a *kārya*. This is the meaning (of the second line of the *kārikā*)

One may argue thus:-

From the usage such as 'it is not done by me, nor is it being done, but it is to be done, it is the future action or the future state existing in the action what is known as *kārya*. This he refutes by *Naḅhavisyad* etc.

Śrakṣyati etc. The word *hi* is to be taken in the sense of 'reason'. So the second quarter of the third line (of the *kārikās*) will mean-' since in the case of *śraksyati* ('will create') although there is futurehood in the action favorable to creation there is no *kāryatva* (the nature of ought to be done).

It cannot be argued that it (*bhavisyatkriyā*) is certainly a *kārya* because it is accepted as the expressed meaning of *liṅ*. The rule *kṛtyāśca* (P.3.3.171) enjoins *kṛtya*-suffixes to convey obligatory action and that is what one finds impossible not to do. Therefore, that it is *kārya*. Thus, raising the doubt, he removes it by *kāryam* etc., (in the fourth line). Since it is impossible not to do such acts as going (for sexual enjoyment) to other's wife and the like, there will be contingency of calling those prohibited acts also *kārya* (ought to be done). This contingency is shown by the words *sāmyād eve* etc. (in the fifth line).

Tad etc. (in the fifth line). It (*tat*) means 'therefore'. That *kārya* is both desired as well as the means of that (desired) is stated through *iṣṭa* etc.

Thus, since the *Brahman* can be either *iṣṭa* (desired thing) or *iṣṭasādhana* (the means to obtain the desired thing), there is no harm for it even if the Veda teaches what is associated with *kāryatva* being fit to be done. This is what is meant.

Well, since *iṣṭasādhanata* (the nature of being the means of desired result) is common [23] to the disk of the moon etc., (People) will take effort (to obtain) that (disk).

No. since in a past act (accomplished through action) there is *kāryatā* (the nature of being produced by an action) as understood by you, there will arise the contingency of your being induced to act again for that which already accomplished.

Now, if you say that the knowledge of present *kāryatā* (being fit to be done) is the cause for action then the knowledge of present *iṣṭasādhanatva* is also like that. Both are alike. Therefore, as it is impossible to define the nature of *kārya* (fit to be done) other than the nature of being the means of the desired thing and as there is no proof for its being the meaning of *vidhi,* it is not the meaning of *vidhi.*

That [24] is insignificant because as there arises the contingency of taking effort for having the disk of the moon etc., it is necessary to take the knowledge of being *kṛtisādhya* (accomplishable by action) as the inducer.

Nor can it be argued that the knowledge of present *iṣṭasādhanatā* is the inducer (of a man to an action) and that is not there (in the disk of moon)[25] For, it should be clarified whether, *idānīntanatva* (being present) is an adjective of either the desire or of the object of desire.

If the first[26] (is accepted), then since it is realised by all that even at present there is desire for the result of (obtaining) the disk of moon, the fault (of not being induced for the attainment of the moon) remains unremoved. For the same reason it is not (an adjective of) either the means or the state of being the means (for the desired).

If the last (i.e. the second proposition [27] is accepted) then there will be no effort for (the performance of) sacrifice etc. because the heaven (which is the object of the desire is not at present[28] here and now.

According to our opinion, on the other hand, *idānīntanatva* is an adjective of *kṛti* (effort) and as such there is no fault (of the type stated above) Moreover, the refutation by *Madhvācārya* (in the *Anuvyākhyāna* stated above) such as ***kāryatva*** (being fit to be done) is not of the nature of being produced by action is to be understood (if accepted at all) either in respect of its being the inducer in regard to any effort or of its being the meaning of *vidhi.*

If the first[29] (is accepted) then, as there is no possibility of taking place of any effort without (the knowledge) the nature of being the means to obtain the desired result and because that i.e. *iṣṭasādhanatva*) also is present in the case of going for sexual enjoyment) to other's wife and the like that (i.e. *iṣtasādhanatva*) stands at par with *kāryatāyāḥ pravartakatvam* i.e. being the inducer effort of for an act fit to be done) since the effort for a prohibited act and the presence of the inducer of it cannot be a fault.

There is no point rejecting *kāryatva* being an inducer of effort.

If the last[30] (is accepted) then since that is common to prohibition also amount to a hindrance such as there will be no possibility of connecting the negative particle with that (the meaning of *Vidhi*). That hindrance is equally there in your case [31] also. Therefore, enough of this objection which simply deceives one's disciples (only). This is the way or model (for further argument).

Nṛsiṁhāśarmas, however, say that the meaning of *liṅ* is *iṣṭasādhanatva* only and not the aspect such as *kṛtisādhyatva* also, because that (i.e. *kṛtisadhyatva*) can not be the meaning of any word as such since it can be got through other means,that is to say, it can be obtained from the power of a root ending in a personal suffix. *Liṅ* etc. do have the power of signifying the volitional effort as *laṭ* etc. (have) by virtue of their having the common feature with regard to *tiṅtva* (i.e. being the personal suffixes). That volitional effort must have some object. Since that effort takes the meaning of the adjacent root as the object and that the object of volitional effort is *kṛtisādhya*, the aspect such as *kṛtisādhyatva* is automatically got.

It cannot also be argued that since *sādhyatva* etc. will manifest (in the *śabdabodha* produced by a *tiṅanta* form) in a *saṁsargatā* manner being a relation between the two word-senses namely *dhātvartha* and the *kṛti*) and not in a *prakāratā* manner, because it is not a word-sense, so there cannot be any desire to act (for *dhātvartha*), because it has been established elsewhere that then only the knowledge and desire are in cause-and-effect relationship where they have the same thing for their adjunct.

Moreover, as in the case of *pacati* (the *śābdabodha* is *pākānukūlā kṛtiḥ*, volitional effort causing cooking) similarly here (in the case of *yajeta* also the *śābdabodha* would be as *yāgānukūlā kṛtiḥ*, 'volitional effort causing performance of sacrifice' and not as *yāgaḥ kṛtisādhyaḥ*,'a sacrifice which can be performed by volitional effort'. Thus, certainly there will not arise any desire (for action). Moreover, sincee the injunctive *kṛt* viz., *kṛtya* suffixes etc., do not have the power of signifying 'volitional effort' there is no scope of having the knowledge of *kṛtisādhyatva* and hence there will be no desire for action.

(The above objection that there will be no desire for action since there is no knowledge of *kṛtisādhyatva* possible does not stand) because the mind will produce such knowledge afterwards. In other words, the knowledge of *kṛtisādhyatva* is possible from the inference such as 'sacrifice can be performed by my effort because it does not possess any property contrary to that of being accomplished by my volitional effort'. Their contention (*Nṛsimhāśrama*'s idea) is this: If *kṛtisādhyatva* alone though known from the veda is not the inducer (of a man to take action) because in that case one who is not capable of performing the sacrifice will also take action (whereas no such man does so). Therefore, the *kṛtisādhyatva* should be qualified by the aspect 'mine' i.e., (being accomplishable by my volitional effort) is the inducer. But since that (*matkṛtisādhyatva*) can be known even from the worldly means, such as observation of performance (of the sacrifices), of *vidhi* can not be taken as signifying that because that can be known by other means and because it is impossible on the part of the vedic *vidhi* to convey (as *śakyārtha*) the aspect 'mine' also i.e., to convey *matkṛtisadhātva*. In fact, the knowledge of *kṛtisadhyatva* is not the inducer. Not taking any effort for a thing which is not accomplishable by action, however, is due to dislike (towards that thing)arising out of a feeling that 'it is laboursome for nothing because it does not yield the desired result'. Therefore, it (*kṛtisādhyatva*) is not the meaning of *liṅ*.

Nor can it be argued that since there is desire to do and in order to justify it, *kṛtisādhyatva* is to be accepted as the meaning of *liṅ*, because that (*kṛtisādhytva*) can be known from the worldly usage.

It cannot be argued that if *iṣṭasādhanatva* also has no *pravartakatva* (the nature of inducing one to act) and not taking any effort for an action which is the means for an evil result and which is indifferent is due to dislike (about that action) arising out of a feeling that 'it is a labour for nothing because of the maxim "every action is troublesome", because it is necessary to assign *pravartakatva* to that (*iṣṭasādhanatva*) on the ground that one does not take any effort for an action which is not the means for the desired even though one has no dislike for the intermediate labour. Moreover, being a means of the desired result means being a means of (obtaining) the object of desire. There, the state of being the meaning (of *liṅ*) is as such, namely, the means of (attaining) heaven etc. (*svargādisādhanatva*) since the knowledge of it being as such is the inducer and not as such namely, (unspecified) *iṣṭatva*, because there is no necessity of the knowledge of desire (for taking effort for the desired thing since the desire by its mere existence is the cause (for taking effort).

Although in the world in the case of effort by force e.g., due to the order of a teacher one (such as a pupil) does take effort for an act knowing that '(the teacher) is inducing me to an action because he knows that there is something good (for me)', still since in the case of something which is accomplishable at the cost of huge wealth and effort and which will be obtained after death, there cannot be any volitional effort without the knowledge of that namely the desired in its particular aspect (like heaven etc.). So the *vidhi* must express the particular aspect of (*iṣṭa* and therefore it is proper to accept only the particularised significative power of that (*liṅ*). For the same reason particular aspect is needed in cases like the said one though there is seen volitional effort in the world in spite of the presence of doubt about the result. There the desire conveyed by the *iṣṭa* acts as the factor which unites all the delimiting adjuncts of being *śakyārtha* in order to remove polysemy of the *liṅ* as in the case of the pronoun *tad* etc. [32]

Thus, the state of being the means of (obtaining) heaven etc. is certainly the meaning of *liṅ* since it cannot be had by any other means.

It cannot be, however, argued that since this (i.e. the state of being the means of (obtaining heaven etc.) also can be known from the association with the words *svargakāma* etc. there is the state of knowing it by other means, because although 'heaven etc. can be known from the compound world ending in (the component) *kāma*, there is nothing to indicate that sacrifice is the means of obtaining heaven etc. and also because in certain injunctive sentences such as *viśvajitā yajeta* (one should perform the sacrifice called (*viśvajit*) there is no association with the compound words ending in such as *svargakāma* etc. This should be borne in mind.

Now, if it is argued that in order to prevent one from taking effort in eating rice mixed with honey and poison the knowledge of not being a cause of greater harm has to be accepted as the cause of volitional effort consequently that (not being a means of greater harm) also will be the meaning of *liṅ*. It is not true because in that case there will be the contingency of taking no volitional effort in something which is accomplishable with very much effort since in that case very many difficulties are bound to occur. Moreover, it is difficult to define the nature of being 'greater' which will pervade throughout, because even (what you will call a little trouble will be a great trouble in comparison to some other still little troubles and therefore a strong dislike for the respective trouble with which something is accomplishable is independently the deterrent factor (of volitional effort) and so it is not proper to postulate that the knowledge of the state of not being the cause of greater harm is the meaning of *liṅ*. Therefore, this is to be noted that one who has strong dislike for the intermediate labour (performing the sacrifice) does not take effort in performance of the sacrifices such as *jyotiṣṭoma* etc. whereas other (who does not have such dislike) does take effort in that.

Nṛsiṁhāśramas, however, say that the state of not being the cause of greater harm is not the meaning of *liṅ* because the knowledge of being the means of greater harm is the deterrent factor (in taking effort). The absence of that deterrent factor alone is needed for the effort. There is no need for the knowledge of absence of being the means of that greater harm) (as the inducer). It can be shown by logical reasoning that knowledge even though it does not disrupt or spoil the cause can be a deterrent factor (with reference to the result). Otherwise, when there is no cause (because it is spoiled or destroyed) there will be no effect (and as such) there is no point in calling that as the deterrent factor (with reference to the effect).

This requires reconsideration, because it is known to all that even knowing that going for sexual enjoyment to other's wife will lead to greater harm, when people have no dislike for that, they take effort for that, and because there is no proof that knowledge of being means of greater harm is the deterrent factor since not taking of any effort is possible due to dislike accepted as a deterrent factor because of the fact that when there is dislike, there is the hindrance to volitional effort as stated above. Therefore, the state of being a means of the desired thing is the meaning of *liṅ*.

Prābhākaras hold that the state of being the means of the desired thing is not the meaning of *vidhi* because as the sacrifice is known as momentary not lasting long, it cannot express that (*iṣṭasādhanatva*), since sacrifice will not be there (as the cause of heaven). Nor can it (*liṅ*) indicate it being indirect means because at a time when, there is no knowledge of an indeterminate cause in a *śābdabodha* the knowledge of *yogyatā* (fitness) is the cause, and *yogyatā* means the state of having the property admitting or establishing the relationship of the adjoining word-sense.

Nor can it be argued that let *sādhanatva* (being a means) be indicated (by *liṅ*) in its general aspect because when there is the amusement of one particular aspect, the knowledge in general necessarily becomes reduced to the state of having the adjuncts other than that (particular aspect).

Moreover, sacrifice is not known (from sentence like *jyotiṣṭamena svargakāmo yajeta* etc.) as something to be done because it is an established maxim that people desirous (of something) understand as only that to be done which is other than the desired one and which is the means that is immediately preceding [33] that desired thing and thus, only the *apūrva* which is the means that immediately preceds the desired (heaven) and which is the intermediary cause (of that desired heaven) can be the meaning (of *liṅ*) as something to be done. *Kāryatva*, after all, means being the aim of volitional effort. There (i.e.,in *kāryatva*) since the volitional effort which is the adjunct requires a substratum and an object, the sacrifice is correlated as the object of it and the person desirous of heaven is correlated as its substratum because as from the practical world it is known that happiness, freedom from sorrows etc. are the aim of volitional effort similarly *apūrva* also is indicated by the Veda as the aim of that since there is no scope of even any doubt of inauthenticity in the Veda which is not man-made.

The state of being an aim is a different property. Thus, since it is impossible to correlate the word *svargakāmaḥ* which is in the nominative with that which is to be done the correlation is made available by changing *sargakāmaḥ* to *svargakāmasya* by extension of the force of that *vidhi*, on the basis of the *upādānapramāṇa*[34]. That is why it is stated in the commentary of *Varadarāja* on *Nayaviveka* that a word expressing its primary meaning has also its primary function extended to the intended meaning of it i.e., the word *svargakāma* proposes to mean the person to be induced (to perform the sacrifice) which is a step further. Thus, the *śābdabodha* (from *svargakāmaḥ yajeta*) will be the inducement with reference to one who is desirous of heaveen has as its object the sacrifice.

Here, that *apūrva* has the sacrifice for its object means nothing but its (*apūrva*) being the aim of volitional effort which has sacrifice as its object and with reference to the fact that sacrifice is the object of the volitional effort of that nature (i.e., the volitional effort which has *apūrva* as its aim) the delimiting adjunct of being a correlator is the state of having the *apūrva* as means and the being producer of that (*apūrva*) and that itself is the *yogyatā* as in the sentence *ghaṭena jalam āhara* (fetch water with the pot') (the *yogyatā* of pot with reference to the bringing of water) is the state of being other than that (pot) which has holes. The understanding of this delimiting adjunct of *yogyatā* is, however, due to supplementing the thing (*chidretargahaṭa*). In the case under discussion, of course, that (*yogyatā*) is got by the primary significative power (of word) itself on the basis of the *upādānapramāna*.

Well, if it is accepted that even (that meaning) which is other than the *śakyārtha* is expressed by the significative power (of a word) then there will be no scope for (the operation of) *lakṣanā*.

It is not true because it is accepted that only that word which conveys the correlation with the primary meaning of the word has the capacity of being expressive of all the meanings which will establish the correlation with the primary meaning of that word. In the case of the expressions *gaṅgāyāṁ ghoṣaḥ* ('the village of the cowhards is situated on the bank of the Ganges') since the primary meaning of the word *gaṅgā* cannot be correlated with the existence of *ghoṣa* there) there is no scope for the operation of *upādānapramāṇa*. In the case of the expression *kākebhyo dadhi rakṣyatām* (Save curd from the crows etc.) there is no *ajahatsvārthālakṣaṇā* [35] and therefore, where is the fault in accepting that *svargakāmasya* is the expressed meaning of *vidhi* on the basis of *upādānapramāṇa*?

Thus, one who understands (from *liṅ*) something as to be done by himself is the person to be induced and one how is desirous of a result understands something as to be done by him and therefore, one who is desirous of heaven is the person who is to be induced in an act which will bring him *apūrva*. Thus, since volitional effort of a man aiming at the *apūrva* enjoined or indicated by the Veda is possible the attainment of heaven is also becomes possible as a matter of fact. Therefore, being the means of the desired thing is not the meaning of *liṅ*.

Moreover, the significative power (of *liṅ*) should be taken either as being the means of an object of the desire or as being the means of heaven. The first is not possible because the knowledge of that cannot be the inducer (of man) since the object of the knowledge which induces alone is the meaning of *vidhi*. The second is (also) not possible because in that case many meanings (of *liṅ*) are to be postulated.

If it is argued that the desire is the uniting factor of all the delimiting adjuncts (of the different meanings conveyed by *liṅ*) as in the case of the pronoun *tad*, it is not correct because there (in the case of *tad*) the knowledge of the knowables[36] is the delimiting adjunct. If it is accepted that in the present case also the desire of the knowable (i.e, the heaven) is the uniting factor of the delimiting adjuncts of the meanings, then there will arise the contingency of desireless ascetics' getting no knowledge (from an injunctive sentence) and since heaven etc. is not known before, *svargasādhanatva* cannot be the expressed meaning of *liṅ*.

Moreover, since in the case of injunctive sentence enjoining obligatory and occasional acts[37] the knowledge is such as follows: 'the inducement of one like me, who is affected by *rāhūparāga* (eclipse) and who is pure and living during the prescribed time (for bath, prayer to *sandhyā* etc.) has as its object the bath and *sandhyāvandana*', there is no expectancy of result (for the injunctive sentences mentioned above) there is absence of result. People take effort in a vedic rite aiming at the *apūrva* which is known as the aim (of that rite). That (*apūrva*) alone is directly conveyed by the Veda as the *puruṣārtha* (i.e. the aim of a man).

Thus, in performing *akāmya* rite the result is got as bye-product. In the obligatory rite also since the *apūrva* is the aim, one takes effort in its performance. Therefore, the aim of the volitional effort i.e., the *apūrva* alone is the meaning of *liṅ*.

Here, this is to be considered: It is improper to say that *apūrva* is the meaning of *liṅ* since there is no supporting evidence for it and because one can have the knowledge of being the means of obtaining the heaven which is the cause of inducement even without that (*apūrva*) .

Though it is not possible to know (the sacrifice) as the direct means (of heaven) since it is very well known that the sacrifice is momentary still, there is no difficulty in knowing it as the means in general. If it is argued that when there is the annulment of one particular aspect the knowledge in general is reduced to the state of having the adjuncts other that the (particular aspect) as in the sentence *ghaṭena jalam āhara* ('bring water with the pot'), when the aspect such as 'having a hole is annulled the *ghaṭa* is delimited by the aspect such as 'being other than that which has holes', thc answer would be no, because also in the case under consideration if the sacrifice cannot be the direct means (of heaven), it is possible to known it as the means other that that (direct means) i.e., as the indirect means and for that knowledge there is no necessity of any madiatory.

In case of being the means of this type the delimiting adjunct of being capable (of producing the result) in the factor which acts as the connecting link, and that link, here, is the *apūrva*.

Thus, when by mere significative power or force with regard to the state of being the means of heaven the *apūrva* can be known on the basis of the *upādānapramāṇa* established by its own[38] (significative power), that (*apūrva*) need not be accepted as the meaning of *liṅ*. Otherwise, there will be the contingency of accepting the delimiting adjunct of *yogyatā* also as the primary meaning of a word and in that case it will result in the fault of endless regression.[39]

Moreover, let the knowledge of being the means got from the veda have that sacrifice alone for its object even as being the indirect means; what for one should accept *apūrva* as the meaning of *liṅ*?

Nor can one argue that unless *apūrva* is known, the state of being the indirect means also will be difficult to be known because even accepting that *apūrva* is the meaning of *liṅ*, since *apūrva* is not known before, no significative power (in *liṅ*) can be realised that (*apūrva*) cannot be known from the word (*liṅ*) also. If you argue that somehow that (*apūrva*) can be known either because of its being the meaning of the word *liṅ* through its being a *kārya* (to be done) or because of the fact that without it the result (heaven) cannot be produced it is easy for me also to know, in the same manner, that *iṣṭa* or heaven through the indirect means (of sacrifice)

Similarly, what you said that one understands something as 'to be done' which is other than the desired one and which is the means of and immediately precedes that desired thing is also not correct because the knowledge of being the means of desired thing is simpler than the knowledge of being the means which immediately precedes the desired thing and that is what induces a man in action, and not the other because of cumbrousness and want of evidence. Moreover, will the means immediately preceding the desired thing be either the means of that main (result) or the means of that subsidiary (result) also? If the first is accepted, should it be either known as being that (i.e., being the means of main result) or as mere something (i.e., without being known in its particularised form)? The first is not true because – as *apūrva* is not known before the knowledge of it as such (i.e., as a means immediately preceding the desired) cannot be possible, hence it (*apūrva*) cannot be known as something to be done. The second alternative is also not possible because even after knowing *apūrva* as something to be done, the sacrifice will not be known as something to be done because it is not the direct means of the main result (such as heaven).

The last alternative (i.e., being the means of subsidiary result) is also not acceptable because when the sacrifice itself can be directly known as something which is to be done there will arise the contingency to give up the views that *apūrva* is the meaning of *liṅ*.

It is also not correct to say that since it is seen in the practical world that the knowledge as 'to be done' is the inducer, that alone is the meaning of *vidhi* because that (*kārya*) which is of the nature of being produced by the volitional effort and which resides in the meaning of the root can be the inducer. So there is no possibility to take *apūrva* like that because that type of knowledge (of *kāryatva*) is possible from the practical world itself. All these have already been stated earlier.

Similarly, your objection that since the nature of being the means of the desired (thing) cannot be defined it cannot be the meaning of *liṅ* is also not proper because it is possible for *liṅ* to express *iṣṭasādhanatva* as the pronoun *tad* etc. express the things delimited by *ghaṭatva* ('being a pot') etc. Let us explain it. Thus, the knowledge of the significative power of the words like *tad* etc., with regard to the things consisted of 'potness', 'clothness', etc. known as being the objects of knowledge (of the speaker) is obtained only in such a way that the words like *tad* etc., is capable of expressing those possessed of the factor that delimits the nature of their being the object of knowledge (of the speaker). In the knowledge, the state of being the object of knowledge (of the speaker) is mere by a uniting factor and not a part of the meaning of the word.

Similarly, here also the knowledge of the significative power of *liṅ* etc. is (only) in this form that *liṅ* etc. are expressive of the means possessed of *svargatva* (heavenness) etc. which is the adjunct, delimiting the state of being an object of desire.

Nor is it a fact that here (in the case of *liṅ*) or in the case of the pronoun *tad*, desire or the knowledge of the knowable is included (in their meaning) because even without that (desire or knowledge of the knowable) the knowledge of the significative power (of *tad* and *liṅ*) is possible since *tad* is capable of expressing the thing possessed of the delimiting factor of their nature of being the objects of the knowledge (of the speaker) and *liṅ* is capable of expressing those things possessed of the delimiting factor of their nature of being the objects of the desire.

Even at the time of knowing the meaning of a word as from the pronoun *tad* etc. the knowledge of a particular thing delimited by the delimiting factor of being the object of the knowledge of the speaker due to the context in possible similarly by the power of the adjacent words such as *svarga* (heaven etc. for *liṅ* the particular knowledge such as the means of heaven is possible.

Well, if it is argued that since sorrow also can be the object of the desire of God, the meaning of *liṅ* would be the state of being the means of that (sorrow) also, it is not correct because it is not an objection but it is desired one; it will be stated later.

Therefore, since the knowledge of being the means of the desired (thing) is necessary as being the inducer, that alone is the meaning of *vidhi* and not the *apūrva* because that is not the aim of ordinary people.

The objection that since meaning of *vidhi* is *iṣṭasādhanatva* (and as such no inducement can take place) in performing *sandhyā*-prayer etc. for which no result is mentioned in the injunctive sentence *ahar ahaḥ sandhyām upāsīta*' one should perform *sandhyā* everyday'), the meaning of *vidhi* is not that is wrong because if it is so people will take no effort for that since that has no result and since trouble alone is the result there, and also because for all kinds of effort the knowledge of being the means is the cause.

It cannot be argued that people will take effort aiming at the *apūrva* because if that is the case then taking that (*apūrva*) as the desired result the meaning of *vidhi* as being the means of the desired (thing) is quite apt.

Actually speaking the definition of the aim in result is the state of being the object of desire and being accomplishable by the object of volitional effort and that does not apply to the *apūrva*.

Nor can one argue that let us postulate something else as that (*uddeśyatva*) because there is no evidence for that. Moreover, there is no use for such *uddeśyatva* in producing the volitional effort which is of the nature of some other *padārtha*.

It cannot also be argued that effort will take place even in the case of what is devoid of result because it is enjoined by the Veda, because even if it is enjoined by the thousand Vedas if such is the knowledge that there is no result to be achieved in performing that even a layman will not be induced.

Nor will there be any contradiction with the statement of Lord Krisṇa (in the *Bhagavadgītā*) that "the sacrifice performed by people with a mental resolve that they should perform the sacrifice simply because it is mentioned in a Vedic injunctive sentence without being desirous of any result is a *sāttvīka* sacrifice" because the God himself has said in the eighteenth chapter (of the *Gītā*) that.

"One should not give up performance of sacrifice, making gift and penance; these must be performed. (Because) performance of sacrifice, making gift and penancing are considered to be purifying ones by the wise men. It is my firm and best opinion, O Arjuna!, that all these (three types of) acts one must perform remaining detached and free from the desire of any result."

Thus, it means that although one performs those acts without aiming at any result, still there is result such as removal of impurities and therefore, one who performs those acts giving up the desire of result does get purified.

Therefore, by performing *jyotiṣṭama* etc. even for obtaining heaven etc. the obligatory performance of *jyotiṣṭama* etc. is also thereby accomplished. This is the established conclusion.

Moreover, if it is accepted that the performance of the obligatory rites such as the *sandhyā*-prayer etc., has no result then the statements 'there are the three[40] *sandhyā*s where is based the brahminhood. One who does not perform them is not called a brahmin', and 'Those who have taken the vow (i.e. every day) to perform always the *sandhyā* become free from sins and go to the external world of *Brahman*' would be purposeless.

If it is argued that the above-mentioned two statements are purposeful as their being the praisess of *sandhyāvandana*, then the sentences *sarvebhyaḥ kāmebhyo darśapūrṇamāsau* 'the *darśa* and *pūrṇamāsa* sacrifices are for all sorts of the desired' and *sarvebhyaḥ kāmebhyo jyotiṣṭomaḥ* 'the *jyotiṣṭoma* sacrifice is for all sorts of the desired' will have to be taken in the same manner (i.e., these are also to be taken as the praisess of *darśapūrṇamāsa* and *jyotiṣṭama*) because when from the sentences *darśapūrṇamāsābhyām svargakāmo yajeta* ' one desirous of heaven should perform the *darśa* and *pūrṇamāsa* sacrifices' and *jyotiṣṭamena svargakāmo yajeta*' one desirous of heaven should perform the *jyotiṣṭoma* sacrifice' the expectancy of the result is over, those earlier two sentences become purposeless.

One cannot however, argue that since the word *sarvebhyaḥ* (in the above sentences) is in the dative case it must mean some result because as the sentence *urjo'varudhyai* [41] 'in order to get strength' which contains the word (*avarudhyai*) in dative and still which is taken as mere praiser similarly though the sentences under discussion contain the word in dative still they can be praising sentences of the *darśapūrṇamāsa* and *agniṣṭoma* sacrifices.

Moreover, even if one accepts that the sentences are purposeful as being the praisers of the *sandhyāvandana*, what is the purpose of this praise? There is none; and therefore, the contingency that these sentences are purposeless cannot be avoided.

If one says that the praise is meant for stimulating it is not true because that too is of no use.

If one argues that the result of that stimulating will be the volitional effort of man, it is also not correct because that is not possible in the case of one who knows the unauthoritativeness of an *arthavāda*, as in the case of one who knows the unauthoritativeness of the sentence shch as *bahudugdheyaṁ gauḥ* (This cow gives lot of milk) uttered by unbelievable person, does not have volitional effort for obtaining that cow.

Well, if it is said that although those sentences referring to the *sandhyāvandana* do not have authority with regard to the purpose of heaven, still they do have authority with regard to the knowledge such as 'they are *arthavādas* because they are expressive of praise (of the *sandhyāvandana*), it is not true because nowhere a praise other than the nature of producing a particular result in question is postulated. Since the knowledge of praise of other qualities (than the quality being productive of the desired thing) cannot be the inducer. If that which cannot produce a particular result also is taken as being productive of that (producing result) and thereby as mere praise by secondary implication.

People will have no faith or regard for the Veda as they do not have regard for the composition of a poetaster. Therefore, they are authority in their literal meaning itself. Thus, in the sentence *sandhyām upāsīta* 'one should perform *sandhyā*' though the desired thing can be known from the *liṅ* it is to be understood that it is an *arthavāda* for the sake of special effort through its being directly indicative of that result through its being indicative of quick production of result. That is why *Kumārila Bhaṭṭa* has said under the *purvapakṣa-sūtra* of the section called *sarvaśaktyadhikaraṇa* such as one who is capable of performing all the accessories should take effort in performing a rite because that rite is prescribed as such with all its accessories because the desired thing which is to be accomplished is common to both (a *kāmya* as well as an obligatory rite). It is explained: 'as a *kāmya-karma* is enjoined for some result similarly a *nitya-karma* is also enjoined for some result; this is the meaning of the above *sūtra*. Thus, according to the view that the nature of being the means of the desired result alone is the meaning of *liṅ*, this [42] is not a drawback.

Now, if being the means of the desired thing is accepted as the meaning of *liṅ* then in the sentence *jyotiṣṭamena svargakāmo yajeta* ('one, desirous of heaven, should perform the *jyotiṣṭama*-sacrifice') the word *jyotiṣṭama* cannot take instrumental case-termination because that is enjoined only if instrumental case is not expressed by anything else. If this is the objection the following is the answer:

As it is going to be stated later (in the next chapter called *subarthanirṇaya*) that the meaning of accusative, instrumental, and locative case-endings is the substratum, that of ablative case-ending is the fixed point (*avadhi*), that of dative case-ending is the thing in view (*uddeśya*), and that of genetive case-ending is the relation or that of all case-endings is the potency alone, it is known that when substratum etc., are not expressed by something else then the substratum as well as the power residing in that substratum receive instrumental and other case-endings. (Similarly) here also although the state of being the means (of the desired thing) is expressed by *liṅ*, since that (substratum of *sādhanatva* i.e., the *sādhana*) is not expressed by *lin*, there is no difficulty to put *jyotiṣṭama* in the instrumental.

What *Mādhavācārya* replied to the above objection that although being the means of the desired thing present in the meaning of the root *yaj* in general which is its own adjacent base, is expressed by the *liṅ* yet since that (*iṣṭasādhanatva*) present in the meaning of the base *jyotiṣṭama* which is of the form of a particular sacrifice is not expressed by it, there is no difficulty in putting *jyotiṣṭama* in the instrumental is wrong because it is difficult to avoid the *sādhanatva* of *jyotiṣṭama* being expressed by the *liṅ* since both *jyotiṣṭama* and the meaning of the root (i.e. the sacrifice) are identical. Otherwise, in the case of the sentence *devadattaḥ pacati* (Devadatta cooks) also although the agent in general is expressed by the *tiṅ* but since the agent in particular i.e., *devadatta* is not expressed by it there is the contingency of using the agent (*devadatta*) in the instrumental (such as *devadattena*).

Others accept that agenthood etc. are expressed by the personal suffixes and explain *anabhihita* as *kartṛtvādāv anabhihite* ('when agenthood etc. are not expressed by some other thing but they say that even though being the means (*kāraka*) in general is expressed (by the *liṅ*) but as the particular *sādhanatva* such as the *karaṇatva* is not expressed by it, there is no harm in putting *jyotiṣṭama* in the instrumental and this is clearly mentioned in the commentary *vivaraṇa* at the end of the first *varnaka* (explanation) in the introductory portion of the *Brahmasūtrabhāṣya.*

The explanation by the *Mīmāṁsaka* and *Naiyāyika*s of *anabhihita* as *anabhihita-saṁkhyāka* ('when the number is not expressed by the *tiṅ*) because agent etc. are not the meanings of the personal suffixes (according to them), and so since the number is in agreement with the agent (*svargakāmaḥ*), agent is assumed to be expressed by the *liṅ* and not the instrument (and therefore, instrumental case-ending can be added to *jyotiṣṭama*)– is unworthy of acceptance, because it will entail the *kṛdanta* forms just as *pacano'gninā pacanī sthālyām* since the number of *karaṇa* and *adhikaraṇa* is not expressed in the above cases.

If it is accepted that *anabhihite* means 'when either instrumentality etc. or their number is not expressed so that the *kṛdanta*-forms such as * *pacano'gninā* [43] (the fire with which one cooks) or * *pacanī sthālyām* [43] (the vessel in which cooking is done) could be avoided, still here also though the number of *jyotiṣṭama* is not expressed by the *liṅ* the instrumentality is certainly expressed and so the instrumental case-ending cannot be had.

One cannot argue that in order to place a *kṛt* suffix on the same level with a *tiṅ* suffix, where the knowledge (of a sentence) has agent as its principal idea or where the intention of a speaker is to refer to the agent as principal, there the agent is assumed to be expressed by *kṛt* or *tiṅ* and here also since the intention of the speaker is not to refer to the instrument as the principal idea of knowledge, the instrumentality is not expressed (and therefore, the above contingency has no scope) because the *śābdabodha* is not restricted to one type only since it depends on the various opinions and because the intention of a speaker which is of the nature of a particular desire is also not fixed because of the maxim: 'the nature of being hateful and that of being desired are not in one-is-to-one relation i.e., uncertain and because this is the experience [44] of the practical world. And if it is so then these will arise the contingency of the unauthoritativeness of the *śāstras*. This is the sum and substance of our discussion.

Now, being the means (of heaven) is to be understood in *jyotiṣṭama*[45]; but that is not possible because heaven is produced by the sacrifice called *vājapeya* also and therefore, *jyotiṣṭama* fails to be an antecedent with regard to the heaven[46]

Nor, one can argue that being the means of a different kind of heaven is to be understood in the *jyotiṣṭama* because the variety could be known only after the production of heaven. The answer to this is stated as follows:

The *liṅ* expresses the state of being the means of a different kind of the desired things. Nor can there arise any doubt with regard to the nature of being means. And the idea of differentness is got from the *liṅ* itself because it is accepted by us that *liṅ* possesses that meaning. For this very reason we had already said before that the potency of *vidhi* is in being the means of a particular result.

Just as the sentence *kambugrivādimān nāsti* (there is nothing having three lines in the neck etc. i.e., there is no pot) according to the view that cumbrous properties (of a thing) are not the delimiting adjunct the counter correlativeness delimited by potness is the relation (between the pot and the non-existence of it). Similarly, here also, the non-existence of being the delimiting factor of the counter-correlativeness of the absolute non-existence co-existing with the heaven is realised (in *jyotiṣṭamatva*) in the relation such as being that which correlates the counter-correlativeness delimited by the state of being the delimiting factor to the absolute non-existence co-existing with the different type of heaven and hence there is no difficulty for *jyotiṣṭama* being the means of heaven. And the theory that the counter-non-existence should have the state of being a correlater of the counter-correlativeness delimited by the delimitor of being a correlative as its adjunct is applicable only in that sentence which contains a negative particle and therefore, there should be no objection (for the above-mentioned relationship). This way Ramakrisṇabhaṭṭacārya has replied.

By the word *svargakāmaḥ* (desirous of heaven) that the heaven is accomplished by *jyotiṣṭama* is not understood as being delimited by hevenness because *liṅ* has no capacity to convey that part of being the delimiting factor (such as heavenness) and because it is impossible too, since heavenness exists even in that which is not produced by that (*jyotiṣṭama*) such as in the heaven produced by *Vājapeya* and therefore , heavenness is over-applied; but what is understood from the *liṅ* is simply the co-existence of heavenness and the state of being accomplished by *jyotiṣṭama*. Here, the knowledge of *vyabhicāra* (such as heaven is produced not only by *jyotiṣṭama*, but also by *vājapeya* etc.) does not stand in the way (of the above-mentioned knowledge from *liṅ*) because the knowledge of *vājapeya* having a particular adjunct is opposed to the knowledge of a–*vyabhicāra* having the same adjunct. Thus, since there is the contingency of knowing *vyabhicāra* in accepting *jyotiṣṭamajanyatva* as pervasive of heavenness you need not accept *jyotiṣṭama* delimited by that (heavenness) as always existing before the effect i.e., the heaven. But there is no harm in accepting causality in *jyotiṣṭama* in relation to that which is the abode of that (heavenness).

Or, the doubt of *vyabhicāra* is not the deterrent factor; on the contrary, that is favorable (for knowing the causality in *jyotiṣṭoma*) because that (doubt) amounts to the doubt about the *yogyatā* (fitness). From the doubt regarding that type of class *jyotiṣṭamatva* there can be no ascertainment of the absence of that (*jyotiṣṭoma*)

Even then, if the delimiting factor of the effect is not known how can the causality be known? If this is your question, the answer is there is 'no' occasion for such question, because as in the case of *parārthānumāna* the invariable concomitance is known from the words even when there is absence of the knowledge of co-existence of probans and prabandum, similarly, here on the basis of the result (heaven) the causality is known. This is what is accepted (by all) Due to the same in some cases of perception where there is nothing to indicate that delimiting adjunct that causality is known as in the case of grass, wood, and the gem which produce fire[1].

Due to the said reason itself, although the delimiting adjunct of the pervaded (smoke) is not known, the knowledge of invariable concomitance in the smoke known as not other than the smoke and light experienced by all is appropriate. Moreover, when the factors for the knowledge of invariable concomitance such as observing the co-existence of probans and probandum are there, nowhere the absence of result is seen simply because of the absence of the knowledge of that delimiting adjunct of pervadedness. Therefore, there is nothing wrong, (in knowing causality in *jyotiṣṭama*)

This view requires reconsideration. In fact producibility means the state of having the delimiting adjunct of that (producibility) and therefore, how can it (producibility) be known without knowing its delimiting adjunct? Also because of the presence of the different factor such as the knowledge of *vyabhicāra* it is impossible to know that.

It cannot be argued that there is no such obstacle in the case of verbal testimony, because it cannot be even thought of that the knowledge of *vyabhicāra* which is of the nature of the ascertainment of the absence of fitness is not the deterrent factor.

Nor can it be argued that there is no ascertainment of *vyabhicārajñāna* and that the doubt about the *vyabhicāra* is not a deterrent factor was already said because when at first it is learnt that heaven is produced by *agnihotra* from the sentence containing the word *agnihotra* (even before knowing it from the sentence containing *jyotiṣṭama*) it is impossible not to have ascertainment about the *vyabhicāra*. Moreover, according to your view evidently the distinction (among the various types of heaven produced by various sacrifices) is not known even superficially before (the various types of heavens are produced). In the case of grass etc. (which are the causes of fires only on account of knowing the distinction, one gets the knowledge of causality from the positive and negative concomitance of a specific thing. Another defect will also be stated later.

Here in the expression *jyotiṣṭamena (svargakāmo yajeta)*, what is understood is: the heaven is absent in that which is different from that which is possessed of *jyotiṣṭama*. It cannot be said that even that is sublated in respect of the delimiting nature of adjunct such as heavenness and so how to know (the causality) because it is possible to know the delimiting adjunct of substratumness in the relationship of their being co-existent. Otherwise, the usage such as *gangāyāṁ na matsyaḥ* (there is no fish in the Ganges) will be unacceptable. Thus, the meaning of *liṅ* is that which has the desired one to be accomplished by it and the state of being to be accomplished is of the nature of the following : at the presence of something, what exists at the next moment and at the absence of the same thing what does not exist at the next moment. That is why in the case of volitional effort for the rites for atonement is justifiable as those rites do not produce the prior non-existence sorrows.

According to the view that being the means (of the desired) is the meaning of *liṅ* since it is impossible to know the causality such as being invariably present before that (*sādhya*), there will be no volitional effort.

One cannct argue that from the knowledge of being the means (alone) there will not be volitional effort because the *sādhyatva* can also be automatically known by the same knowledge of being the means, and thereby the volitional effort is possible. This is what the new logicians say.

This is what is to be noted:

During the knowledge of *vyabhicāra* regarding the co-existence of smoke and the ass although some smoke absent in that which is other than that which is devoid of the ass is known, still it is well-known to all that no-body takes any effort to collect the ass and therefore, since such a knowledge is not the inducer, *sādhyeṣṭatva* is not the meaning of *liṅ*. Moreover, if what you say is accepted, there will be no necessity of postulating difference in the result. Since at the very beginning the inducing knowledge is established there is no basis to postulate difference in the result.

It cannot, however, be argued that it is necessary to postulate that difference in order to justify the causality known before, because even without the generic quality there is no difficulty in knowing that heaven is produced by the sacrifice, and because the universal is not the cause of the nature of causality. Nor is its utility for knowing the causality because in the present case itself (according to you) it is not there. The generalisation that like causality effectness also must be delimited by some delimiting adjunct is unacceptable (to us).

When such is the position then why not the heaven produced by the *aśvamedha* be produced by the *jyotiṣṭama*? No. (Such question should not be put) (since one may equally ask) even though the difference is postulated (in heaven) why not the heaven produced by a particular *jyotiṣṭama* be produced by another *jyotiṣṭama*? Because if (the answer is) this is the nature of things or for a particular heaven a particular sacrifice is the cause then from the very beginning you should have followed that (method);

what is the use of (hunting for) the delimiting factor such as the generic quality (heavenness)?

Therefore, you must accept that effect is of the nature of being the possessor of the delimiting adjunct of the effectness and that is difficult to know without knowing the delimiting adjunct.

Or let heavenness be the delimiting factor. My father has said in the *Advaitasāroddhāra* the way how a quality even if it is over-applied - can very well be the delimiting factor.

In the *Advaitasāroddhāra* while refuting the generic quality such as substanceness (your father) has answered others : let, there be the 'sacrifice' as the delimiting factor of the state of being the inherent cause removing the argument that the state of being the inherent cause of effect in general must have a delimiting factor. Unless we accept a universal running through all substances, we cannot have the causality suitably delimited.Hence substanceness gets established.

One should not ask that if existence is accepted as the delimiting factor of being the inherent cause then there is the contingency of colour being produced in quality (since quality also has the delimiting factor 'existence') because for the production of a particular colour a particular inherent cause is required and so in the absence of a particular cause there will be absence of a particular result. Therefore, what he said may be appropriate.

But you have said that the delimiting adjunct of effectness (such as heavenness) may be over-applied. That is wrong because if it is so the heaven delimited by heavenness cannot be produced by *Agnihotra* because of the absence of its cause such as the *jyotiṣṭama*. If you argue that inspire of that (contingency) heaven can be produced, then as in the case of the production of pot as ass is not the cause because of *vyabhicāra* similarly *jyotiṣṭama* etc. cannot be the cause of heaven. If you say so, the answer is as follows: When either *vrīhi* or *yava* enjoined with reference to the *darśapūrṇamāsa* by the injunctive sentences *vrīhibhir yajeta* (one should perform the sacrifice with *vrīhi*) and *yavair yajeta* (one should perform the sacrifice with *yava*) independently is capable of producing the result and as no *vyabhicāra* is accepted there in producing the effect by either of the two causes, similarly here also let any one (of the sacrifices such as *jyotiṣṭama*, *angnihotra*, *vājapeya* etc.) produce the heaven. It cannot be argued that both *vrīhi* and *yava* are causes (of heaven) because of their being the possessor of the same power (to produce the heaven) and because of their being either (of the two causes of heaven). Because of the contingency of going against the established conclusion that the two mantras– one expressing the preparation of the seat for the sacrificial cake and the other expressing placing of the cake on that seat such as *syonaṁ te sadanaṁ kṛṇomi ghṛtasya dhārayā suśevaṁ kalpayāmi* (I am preparing a beautiful seat for you and soothening it with the flow of ghee) and *tasmin sīdāmṛte pratitiṣtha vrīhīṇāṁ medha sumanasyamāna* (you sit there and be there, O oblation made of *vrīhis*! O tender-minded !) are the accesory (i.e. are to be recited) when the cake is made of *vrīhi* alone and not when it is made of *yava* on the basis of the words : *vrihīṇām medha*;

There itself since there is the contingency of either non-production of the effect (heaven) produced through *apūrva* or *vyabhicāra* if a difference is postulated in *apūrva* and thereby the fixing up of the optional use of the two *mantras* is justified then there will arise the contingency of non-applicability of *saṁskāras* of *vrīhis* to *yavas* like (the non-applicability of) the *saṁskāras* of the *soma*-cups sush as cleaning etc. to the '*camasas*' square wooden vessel taking into account the *somāpūrva*, the being means of the contextual *apūrva* got through the suggestive power is common to the *camasa*, If it is said that from the word *graha* (soma-cup) *avāntarāpūrva* (intermediate-*apūrva*) (alone) is immediately known being the closest one and hence the *camasas* are excluded, similarly from the word *vrīhi* also since the particular *apūrva* accomplishable by the *vrīhis* is known, the non-applicability of *saṁskāras* such as sprinkling etc. to *yavas* cannot be avoided.

Therefore, causality of *vrihis* and *yavas* is to be understood with reference to the same type of *apūrva* only. Similarly, grass, wood and *yavas* are causes with reference to their effect, fire.

It cannot be argued that if that is accepted then the ass also would have to be treated as the cause of (producing) the pot, if on the basis of *vyabhicāra* it is rejected, then grass etc. also are to be rejected as causes since there is no proof to establish the causality (of the ass with reference to the pot).

The causality of *yava* etc. with reference to *apūrva* is established by the Veda and that of grass etc. (with reference to fire) is established by direct observation along with the reasoning of pros and cons such as in a heap (of grass) devoid of a particular wood and grass if grass is there there is fire and if there is no grass there is no fire. In the case of ass, however, there is neither of the two to establish that it is a cause (of pot). On the contrary, compared to the necessary postulates such as the stick etc. it (ass) is superfluous and therefore, there is no possibility of its being a cause.

Still, (when it is a fact that) without cause there can be no effect, how, in the absence of *vrīhis* can *yavas* produce the effect *apūrva*? True, but there will be no such fault or defect because the relation such as the vow delimited by the *saṅkalpa*: *vrīhibhir yakṣye* (I shall perform the sacrifice with *vrīhis*) is considered as delimiting factor of the relation effectness of *vrīhis* and since by that relation the effect *āgneyāpūrva* cannot be produced by *yavas*, there is no *vyabhicāra* since *vrīhis* are enjoined by the Veda as the cause only (of such *āgneyāpūrva*).

And since the effect *apūrva* of taking vow becomes extinct after the production of *āgneyāpūrva*, there is no impropriety in using *yavas* on another occasion by the (same) sacrifice. Similarly, grass etc. are also causes with reference to the effect delimited by fireness through the relation of contact delimited by the strawness through the identical relation and strawness. This is what is to the observed.

When *Agnihotra* is the cause of heaven, heavenness is the delimiting factor, (of effectness) through the relation of inherence associated with the *apūrva* produced by the *Agnihotra*. Therefore, that the same type of heaven is produced by *Agnihotra* etc. cannot be prevented. It is stated in the *Taittirīya Saṁhitā* that if a man having known thus performs the *Agnihotra* obtains that such as such is obtained by the *Agniṣṭoma*; if a man having known thus performs the *paurṇamāsī* obtains that such as such is obtained by *Ukthya*; if a man having known thus preforms the *Amāvāsyā* obtains that such as such is obtained by the *Atirātra*. The learned should take note of it. For the said reason alone the statement of the learned men such as the following is apt. "The state of being inferred through the smoke is the delimiting factor of effectness of subsumptive reflection of smoke; but difference in inference is never postulated" forwarded by Mīmāṁsaka etc.

To the view, expressed at the time of discussing the meaning expressed by *liṅ* that if difference (in the result) is not accepted there will arise the contingency of sameness of the result of *Jyotiṣṭoma* and *Agnihotra* and when one can achieve the desired result (i.e. heaven) through *Agnihotra* which can be performed with little expense of wealth and with little effort, there will arise the contingency of not taking any effort (to perform jyotiṣṭoma etc.) because of dislike since that will require more labour (without producing extra result) and so it will amount to the state of inoperation of the Vedic injunctive sentence such as *Jyotiṣṭomena Svargakāmo yajeta, Asvamedhena* yajete etc. Therefore, one must postulate that (difference is result), the following is the answer.

Since the knowledge of causality of the desired (result) is the inducer (of a man) in the case of *Jyotiṣṭoma* also, there will arise no contingency of not causing any effort (for the performance of *Jyotiṣtome* etc.) Moreover, all do not have hatred toward (lobourious and expensive thing) and so one who does not have (dislike) will be induced to perform (those sacrifices). Otherwise, even in the case of your Agnihotra (which is easier to perform) the most lazy person will not take effort (for that) and therefore, the same fault (of imopertive nature of Vedic injunctive sentences) arises (in your view also). Actually speaking, even when there is no difference in the result, people do take effort mistaking about that (difference) i.e. thinking that there may be some difference in the result.

One should not have a doubt that how an erroneous knowledge can induce a man to act since at the time of explaining the Vedic injunctive sentence *svādhyāyo' dhyetavyaḥ* (one should study one's own branch of the Veda) it has been stated that the knowledge produced only by the three *pramāṇas* (such as perception, inference and verbal testimony) is useful for fruitful effort because as knowledge is produced by the body (also) it is not a fact that knowledge is produced by the three *pramāṇas* only.

Here (in the present case under discussion) the theory that knowledge is produced only by the three *pramāṇa* (not by any other pramāṇa) remains unaffected because in the knowledge produced by the Vedic sentence itself there appears to be difference (in result) due to some defect, and the defect cannot be treated as the means of valid knowledge.

Or there is no impossibility of a capable man's taking effort for a labourious and expensive act because he will take effort in order to remove bad name arising from his not performing those costly sacrifices or in order to obtain additional result such as worldly fame. That is why it is said in the *Bhagavadgītā* that (O Arjuna! if you do not go for the war being a Kṣatriya) people will speak permanently ill of you and for a respected man (like you) (getting) bad name is worse than death. Therefore, (you must maintain your) own fame and duty... wherein worldly fame is said to be the factor inducing (a man to act).

For the same reason on the part of Yudhiṣthira and others who were well-versed in all the systems of learning taking effort in killing their kiths and kins and the brahmins for the sake of a meagre result such as the kingdom is justifiable. Therefore, extreme desire to get fame etc. is the inducing factor with reference to taking effort (for an action) and so there is no defect mentioned above (of not taking effort for a costly and laborious sacrifices). For the same reason it is observed that although people today know that no sacrifice is perfectly performed with all its accessories, still for the sake of worldly fame they take effort in an expensive and labourious sacrifice. Because of extreme longing for fame they do not mind the huge expense and labour. Therefore, even if difference(in result) is not accepted there will arise no contingency of not taking effort (in *Jyotiṣṭoma* etc.).

Actually speaking, from the sentence *sarvebhyaḥ kāmebhya darśapūrṇamāsau* (The darśa-pūrṇamāsa sacrifices are for all results) when all sorts of results can be obtained from *Darśa-pūrṇamāsa*-sacrifices you too cannot avoid purposelessness of *putreṣti* etc. If one perform Darśapurṇamāsa sacrifies which are obligatory sacrifices in order to get son etc. it will be established on the strength of *prasaṅga* that he has performed by the obligatory *Darśapūrṇamāsa* also and in order to minimize the labour of performing two sacrifices (such as the obligatory Daśapūrṇamāsa and the *putreṣṭi*) he will not take any separate effort for *Putreṣṭi* etc.

Well, exactly for this reason, some excellence is postulated is the result of the *Putreṣṭi*, It cannot however, be argued that since that excellent (result) also can be had from *Jyotiṣṭoma* itself because it is enjoined also for (getting) son etc. on the basis of the enjoining sentence *sarvebhyaḥ kāmebhyo jyoṭiṣṭomaḥ* (the *jyotiṣṭoma* is meant for all desired result). The contingency of not taking effort (for *Putreṣṭi*) and thus its becoming purposeless is difficult to be avoided. Because it is possible to justify volitional effort for the respective sacrifices in order to get three types of results (from three sacrifices such as *Darśapūrṇamāsa*, *Jyotiṣṭoma* and *Putreṣṭi*) by postulating three kinds of results (to them).

Or, since out of the sentences enjoining sacrifices (such as *Darśapūrṇamāsa* and *Jyotiṣṭoma*) for all desired results, *Darśa* and *Pūrṇamāsa* are enjoined for desired results produced by all *Iṣṭi* only and *Jyotiṣṭoma* is enjoined for the desired result produced by all soma-sacrifice only, there is no possibility even of getting the result produced by *Putreṣṭi* etc. from *Jyotiṣṭoma*. Or, there is no need of postulating three types of results (only two types of difference will do; but difference in result must be accepted).

What you have said so far is not true. Because when it is possible to avoid the fault of purposelessness of *Putreṣṭi* etc. as there is possibility of performing the *Putreṣṭi* before performing the *Darśapūrṇamāsa* on the part of a man who has performed the *Agnyādhāna rite* and who is desirous of a son etc. There is no scope for postulating difference in the results at all because that will be superfluous. One should not argue that since soma-sacrifice is to be performed after the (performance of) *Darśapūrṇamāsa*-sacrifices on the basic of the Vedic injunction *darśapaūrṇamāsābhyām iṣṭvā somena yajeta* (after performing *Darśapaurṇamāsa* one should perform soma-sacrifice), there is no proof in support of any other *Iṣṭi* being prior to soma-sacrifice.

Well, let it be so, our view is not atall affected. But your counter objection that *Putreṣṭi* becomes purposeless has been answered; if we say so then ?

Still we say that for those who have already started performing the *Darśapūrṇamāsa* will have no volitional effort for any *Kāmyeṣṭi*.

In fact it has been settled in the *Agniṣṭomaprakaraṇa* on the authority of the vedic statement such as "One desirous of performing a *Soma*-sacrifice should perform the *Agnyādhāna*-rite. He need not wait for the season or the position of constellation prescribed for it "that for a person who, considering the momentariness of wealth and mind, wants to perform a *Soma*-sacrifice and immediately wants to have the result of it and who has not yet performed the obligatory *Agnyādhāna*, there is no need to wait till the prescribed time for *Kāmya Agnyādhāna* since one requires fire to perform Agniṣṭoma for that result.

Thus, since *Darśa* and *Pūrṇamāsa*- require a month for their performance, a rich man who has keen desire for the heaven and who is not prepared to wait till that time (i.e. one month) can easily perform *Soma*-sacrifice for the same heaven and thus the purposelessness of *Jyotiṣṭoma* is avoided and so how can the postulation of any abundant excellence of the result such as the heaven be established in *Soma*-sacrifice compared to the *Darśapūrṇamāsa*-sacrifices ? Because, it is very often experienced in this practical world that an object which can be obtained with little expense of wealth and with little effort etc. but with delay in time etc. is achieved (by people), if there is extreme desire and if they want to obtain it soon - with more expense of wealth and with greater effort etc.

All who will perform *Agnyādhāna* will definitely go to perform the soma-sacrifice and *yakṣyamāṇa* means one who wants to perform *jyotiṣṭoma* immediately after performing the Adhāna. There is no precedence of Agnihotra even for his performing the *Jyotiṣṭoma*. This, also , is to be noted.

Moreover, because of proximity the sentence containing *svargakāma* supplies the result for only the obligatory rites enjoined by the sentences *yāvajjīvam agnihotraṁ juhoti* (one should perform Agnigotra throughout one's life) and *yāvajjīvaṁ darśapaurṇamāsābhyām yajeta* (one should perform *Darśapaurṇamāsa* as long as one lives) and so one need not postulate any result such as 'absence of evil' in obligatory rites. Because compared to postulation of desires such as absense of evil' caused by dislike of that (evil) after knowing the evil, it is easier and proper to postulate the desire of heaven and also because of the rule of Jainini such as "that result may be the heaven because it is commonly desirable to all".

In fact, even if difference in result is not accepted, volitional effort (with reference to *Jyotiṣṭoma*) is possible because the two results of (*Jyotiṣṭoma* and *Agnihotra* will differ (Quantitatively) as being more or less respectively and so there is no contingency of unauthoritaliveness of either. Otherwise, when all the results can be obtained from the *Darśapaurṇamāsa* on the strength of the Vedic statement *sarvebheyaḥ kāmebhyo darśapaurṇamāsau* (*Darśaparṇamāsa* is meant for all desires) how can one prevent purposelessness of other sacrifices (than the *Darśapaurṇamāsa*)?

Actually speaking, even the postulation of quantitative difference in results is not proper because there is no proof for it and also because it will result in cumbrousness. But settlement of the rites which have equal results as per the capacity of their performers (i.e. one who is capable of performing *Jyotiṣṭoma* will perform *Jyotiṣṭoma* and one who is not capable of Performing *Agnihotra* will perform *Agnihotra*. But the result will the same). This is why what is stated in the *Mahābhārata* that "One capable of giving thousand should give (at least) hundred, one capable of giving hundred should give (at least) ten and one as per one's capacity should give simply water. All are said to be of equal result" is apt. This obligation is wanted elsewhere also for all on the basis of the sentences such as one should not be stingy with regard to one's wealth (i.e. with regard to one's capacity to give).

One need not have any doubt that there will arise the contingency of not taking volitional effort with regard to *Darśapaurṇamāsa* for those who are capable of performing *Jyotiṣṭoma* and with regard to *Agnihotra* for those who are capable of performing *Darśapaurṇamāsa*. Because volitional effort is possible (for those sacrifices) on the strength of the obligatory injunctions such as "one should perform *Darśapaurṇamāsa* through out one's life; one should perform Agnihotra throughout one's life". Therefore, there is no need of further elaboration.

Moreover, let us accept difference (in results) in order to justify volitional effort (with regard to different sacrifices); still it amounts to the fact as objected by you before that as mere knowledge of being the means of desired object is not the inducer (of a man in action) so is the knowledge of being the means of heaven in general; but the knowledge of being the means of a particular result alone is the inducer. Thus, although it is known that the producibility by *Aśvamedha* etc. is co-existent with heavenness and although it is known that (heavenness) does not exist in what is other than that which possesses *Aśvamedha* still volitional effort is not possible and so on the part of *vidhi* to produce knowledge of that sort is also purposeless. Because that alone is the meaning of *vidhi* which is the object of the knowledge which induces (a person to act) and therefore, (what you say) is not worthy of taking note of.

The view that the knowledge produced by *vidhi* is not directly the inducer (of a person to act) but some other knowledge caused by that (knowledge produced by *vidhi*) and this is why the author of *Cintāmaṇi* has said that the knowledge produced by the knowledge which is produced by *vidhi* is the inducer is unworthy of acceptance. Because of the rule that the postulation in the absence of different factor, has for its object the direct cause of volitional effort, it is but proper to assume the significative power of *vidhi* as having only that object the knowledge of which directly induces (a man to act). Otherwise, as per the statement of *Udayanācārya* that "*Vidhi* means the intention of a speaker with reference to volitional effort which is expressed by *liṅ* etc.; whereas being the means of the desired object of the doer is to be infered". The significative power of *vidhi* will amount to the intention of the speaker. Because it will be easier to establish (that meaning of *vidhi*) taking the class attribute such as desireness as the delimiting factor. Thus, the theory that being the means of one's desired object is the meaning of *vidhi* is gone. If, however, you insist that the state of being the express meaning of vidhi can be applicable only to that object the knowledge of which directly induces (a man to act), then it is but proper to postulate that the significative power (of *vidhi*) relates to being the means of a particular heaven.

According to our theory when taking volitional effort is possible from the knowledge produced by *vidhi* itself there is no proof in support of postulating the series (of knowledges) of the type mentioned above and that will be cumbersome. Wise men should take note of it.

Even if what you have said is accepted the negation, in the sentence na *kalañjam bhakṣayet* (one should not eat *kalañja*), does not fit. Because eating *kalañja* producees the desired object such as satisfaction (of hunger) etc. and therefore, the absence of that (i.e. causing satisfaction) is barred (i.e. cannot be accepted as a fact).

By this the argument of the author of the *Kalpataru* and others that in order to justify the absence of being the means of desired object expressed (in the above mentioned sentence), the state of being the means of greater evil is postulated (compared to the smaller desire of satisfaction of hunger) is hereby set aside.

It is stated in the *Parimala* that when the state of being the means of greater evil is postulated and when that is noted one will refrain from taking volitional effort with regard to immediate result and once he refrains from that the immediate result is not his desired object and therefore, if the sentence *na brāhmaṇaṁ hanyāt* (one should not kill a brahmin) means absence of being the means of desired object there is no defect in saying so. But (it is a fact that) a person who believes in god and the other world and who is lustful, in spite of his having the knowledge of the sorrows of the hell which are sure to happen, does not get rid of the desire for the immediate result and thus to him there is the contingency of a negative sentence which means the absence of being the means of desired object, being unauthoritative.

It is not proper to say that authoritativeness and unauthoritativeness of the Veda will vary from person to person when (it is an established fact) that the veda is authoritative to all and therefore, the author of the *Parimala* himself sets aside this and posits the state of not being the cause of greater evil also as the meaning of *vidhi*. Thus, negation of the qualified (1) tantamoumiting to the negation (2) of the qualification is conveyed by the negative particle and so there is no fault. This also is set aside in the manner stated above. Therefore, how is it (i.e. how can the meaning of *vidhi* such as *iṣṭasādhanatva* fit in the negative construction)? They answer as follows : the state of not being the cause of greater evil done, known as being the correlater of being the means of desired object in the sacrifice etc. through the secondary power or effected by illusion, is negated and therefore, as in the case of the words, *asurā*, *avidyā* etc. (the opposite meaning is expressed) similiarly, there also (i.e. in the case of *na kalañjam bhakṣayet* etc.) evil alone is known (as the meaning of the negative sentence). This is what others say.

One need not take any objection that as in the case of *asurā and avidyā* there should be negative compound in the case of *na kalañjan bhakṣayet* also. Because that (compounding) is optional on the strength of the governing rule *vibhāṣā* (P.2.1.11). Hence, in the sentence *nānuyājeṣu yeyajāmaham karoti* where *paryudāsa* is the meaning, there is no compounding. This has already been stated in the earlier section (*Dhātvarthanirṇaya*).

According to the view that being the means of a particular (result) is the meaning of *vidhi* it is accepted that the word *svarga* (heaven) etc. is expressive of the particular result and in that case (in a negative sentence) being the means of evil is the meaning of 'liṅ' and the negative particle is indicative of the intention(of the speaker). This is what others propose.

As per the view that being the means of a particular (result) is the meaning of *vidhi*, in the sentence *na kalañjam bhakṣayet* being the means prior to non-existence of averting evil is the meaning of *vidhi*. And being the means, here, means the consideration of pros and cons such as in the presence of that (i.e. not eating of *kalañja*) invariably there is absence of evil and in the absence of that (i.e. eating of *kalañja*) invariably there is evil.

The evil also is to be understood as different because of its being different from the sentence *na brāhmaṇam hanyāt* (one should not kill a brahmin). Thus, the negation of the meaning of *vidhi* alone is done by a negative particle. And thus if eating of that (*kalañja*) is there evil is bound to be there. Therefore, there is no difficulty (in fitting the meaning of *vidhi* in a negative construction). This is the opinion of some others. That the absence of eating of *kalañja* is the means of averting evil is understood (as the meaning of the sentence *na kalañjam bhakṣayet*).

One need not raise an objection that when suffixes are taken as indicative of their meaning associated with the meaning of their bases how, then, can being the means of desired object (i.e. the meaning of the suffix) be related to the absense (i.e. the meaning of the negative particle) which is not the meaning of its base? Because it is possible to relate that through the absence. Or, in the case of negative particle the postulation of other causation with reference to the *liṅ* etc. which are associated with the negative particle could be adopted. Similarly, in the sentences *atirātre ṣoḍaśînaṁ gṛhṇāti* (one should hold *ṣoḍaśî*-cup in the *Atirātra*-sacrifice) and *nātirātre ṣoḍaśînaṁ gṛhṇāti* (one should not hold *Ṣoḍaśî-cup* in the *Atirātra-* sacrifice) in both holding and not holding (of the Ṣoḍaśi-cup) being the means of the desired object is known. And since there is no difference in result there is no fault (in the *vikalpa*). That is why the Prābhākaras hold the view that *Kārya* (to be done) the object of which is the absence of eating of *Kalañja* is the meaning of *vidhi* (in he sentence *na kalañjaṁ bhakṣayet*). Some have stated like this.

If this is the case then there will arise the contingency of getting sin in killing the *Agniṣomīyapaśu* (the *paśu* meant for Agni and Soma). Because (killing) is prohibited by the injunction *na hiṁsyāt sarvā bhūtāni* (one should not kill any creature.) and because there is no proof to restrict that injunction from operating in the present case (of killing the *Agniṣomīyapaśu*). Thus, from the sentence *Agnīṣomīyam paśumālabheta* it is known that killing (of the *Agniṣomīyapaśu*) is the means of the desired object. And by the sentence *na hiṁsyāt sarvā bhūtāni* it is expressed that (the killing) is the means of evil. There is no contradiction between these two. Because (both being the means of desired object and being the means of evil) are seen contained together in the cases of eating rice mixed with honey and poison and having sexual inter-couere with other's beautiful wife.

In fact, in the sentence *Agnīṣomīyaṁ paśumālabheta* the root *ā-labh* means sacrifice by secondary implication. Because that (sacrifice) which is not enjoined earlier and which contains both the material and the god is enjoined here.

Or, let *ālambhana* mean mere touching (of the beast). Because when the opponent raised the doubt in the section (of the Bhāṣya of Śabara) discussing the sūtra of Jaimini: *Viṣaye prāyadarśanāt* that on the strength of the sentence *Vatsam ālabheta* (one should kill the calf) read in the *Agnihotraprakaraṇa* there will arise the contingency of enjoining killing of the calf it has been concluded that mere touching is the meaning of that (ā + *labh*) for the same reason, the statement of the *Bhōgavatapūrāṇa* that the smelling of wine and the touching of the paśu are enjoined by the Veda and not *hiṁsā* is quite correct.

Moreover, according to the *nyāya* of the *Trivṛccarvadhikaraṇas* that in all cases touching alone is the meaning (of the root, *ālabh*) is established. There having stated *trivṛd bahiṣpavamānam* because the nine verses are stated in the joining passage the word *trivṛt* means a proof of nine verses . In the practical world, on the strength of the usage *trivṛd rajjuḥ trivṛt* means a rope having three threads. The word *caru* means a cooking vessel in the practical world. But in the Veda having stated *Ādityas' caruḥ* (*caru* pertaining to Aditi) is stated *Aditim odanena* (one should please Aditi with cooked rice), therefore, it is decided that *caru* means cooked rice. Even after this decision where there is no mention of the paraphrase, there, in the case of *trivṛd agniṣṭud agniṣṭoma sauryaṁ caruṁ nirvapet* etc. both (vedic as well as popular) the meanings are to be accepted. Even in the case where the paraphrase of a word is seen, both the meanings should be accepted optionally because so far as the indication of meaning of a word is concerned both the veda as well as the worldly usage are equally strong; having raised such doubt it has been decided that one should accept the meaning of the Vedic paraphrase only because it is stronger since it is too close to the vedic injunction. Elsewhere (i.e. where vedic paraphrase of a word is not found) also the vedic interpretation alone is to be accepted since that is also a vedic case. This is what will be stated in the tenth chapter of Jaiminīya work.

Similarly, here too, from the context when touching is settled as the meaning (of ā + *labh*) elsewhere (i.e.out side that context) also the same meaning is to be accepted, this is what is established (from this).

Thus, when there is absence of commonness in the sphere between the injunction and the prohibition where is the question of one being *bādhya* and the other being *bādhaka*? Killing of the animal is however, inferred by the rites of offering of the limbs of animal.

One cannot argue that since the rite of offering of a limb of animal could be performed by the already available limbs of the animal as the *patnīsaṁyāja* is performed by the available tail (of an animal) there is no necessity for killing an animal in the middle of the sacrifice. Because in order to justify these the earlier *saṁskāras* of the animal are meant for the sacrifice through the animal meant for the sacrifice those *saṁskāras* are performed in the middle of the sacrifice as the *saṁskāras* of asking the pady (for the sacrifice) is done. Otherwise, there will arise the contingency of (the limbs to be offered) not being the (limbs of) the *Agniṣomīya* animal.

From the sentences enjoining the process of cutting he limbs (of the sacrificial animal)the cutting (of the animal) is known. Otherwise (i.e. if the already cut limbs of the animal is procured and offered to the fire then) there will be the contingency of performance of the (animal) sacrifice (with the parts of the animal) killed by the cutting knife etc. also.

No. in order to get the uncut particular limb (of the animal for offering) and in order to keep away the fault of crying (of the animal) the process of killing the animal becomes purposeful and therefore, the injunction *Agniṣomīyaṁ paśumālabheta* (one should kill the Agniṣomiya animal for offering) does not require the injunction of killing. This is the fact.

It is not a proper way to say that since what is enjoined by the injunctive sentence not accompanied by any sentence expressive of evil result or injunction of atonement is pervaded by the state of not being the cause of any evil and since there will be direct conflict with the resulant meaning of *vidhi* (of the prohibition), the prohibition (expressed is *na hiṁysyāt sasvā bhutāṁ*) does not operate (in the case of killing the *Agniṣomīya* animal). Because when there is a conflict between two expressed meanings, due to the fear that one of these two may turn unauthoritative restriction of either is postulated.[1]) But when the conflict is with the resultant meaning of the *vidhi* the veda does not become unauthoritative and so no restriction (of scope of the prohibition could be imposed).

Nor the commentary given by Madhvācārya on the Brahmasūtra : *Aśuddham iti cen na śabdāt* (if you say the scarifies is impure) because of the killing of the animal, let there be misery it is not correct because the killing is enjoined by the Veda.

If you say this, it is incorrect because the killing being as such is not the cause of sin, but being a forbidden thing. Here the state of being forbidden is not only not present, but on the other hand it is enjoined by the words like *Vayavyam svetam ālabheta*

---

1. In the present case, however, the killing is the implsed meaning, whereas prohibition is the express meaning. Therefore, the restriction o the sphere of the prohibitive sentence (*na hiṁsyāt sarvābhūtāni*) in the case of the killing of the Agnisomiya animal cannot be done.

supports this view. It says: "the non-vedic killing will definitely result into evil; but the killing enjoined by the veda never results into evil result (i.e. sin)". This is what is stated in the Bhāṣya. The Bhāṣya is further explained as follows :

Since the killing enjoined by the veda is also after all the killing it is the cause of sin and so let one who performs a sacrifice suffer in the heaven. This doubt is being raised by *aśuddham* etc. A killing is the cause of sin not because it is a killing but because it is prohibited. That prohibition is absent here. To the contrary, that is enjoined by the words *vāyavyaṁ śvetam ālabheta* (one should kill (for the sacrifice) the animal meant for the god Vāyu) etc. This idea is expressed through *śabda* etc.

And the inference (such as the killing enjoined by the veda is the cause of sin, because it is a killing like the killing in the practical world) is fallacious one because it is spoiled by the adventitious condition (*upādhi* such as being prohibited by the veda) and as such that it will go against (the statement) of the smṛti is expressed through the words *hiṁsā* etc.

The whole interpretation is wrong because it is based on not understanding (properly) the idea of the opponent. The opponents do not prove syllogistically sin (in the Vedic killing) because it is killing; but because it is prohibited. For you too who understand *vidhi* as being the means of the desired object the position remains the same. The smṛti (quoted above is mere imagination by *Madhvācārya* who is (famous) in imagining the imaginary *śrutis* such as Kamaṭha etc. and therefore, it is unauthentic. It is to be noted.

Thus, (i.e. if what you say is accepted then) there will arise the contingency of jumping into the Triveṇī, self immolation of a widow with her deceased husband, etc. all being vanished (i.e. no body will following them because they will produce sin according to you). Similarly, in the Vājapeya-Sacrifice one cannot avoid the contingency of sin caused by the taking of liquor. Moreover, it is said in the first skandha of (the *Bhāgavatapurāṇa*) that "as by the mud the water of mud cannot be removed or by liquor as (the sin) caused by taking the liquor cannot be wiped out; similarly, (the sin caused by) one kind of killing of the creature cannot be wiped out by (performing) the sacrifices. If this is your (objection) the following is the answer to this objection.

(The king tells the demoness called *karkaṭi* that after finishing (i.e. eating up) the first lot of bad people you can come again and) "can take other persons worthy of being killed (because) according to the religion there will be no *hiṁsā* in their killing. And a killing which is as per one's duty is equal to great compassion". This is what is stated in the Yogavāṣiṣtha in the *Karkaṭyupākhyāna*.

In the Uttarakhaṇḍa of the *Brahmapurāṇa* in the chapter narrating the advice given by verify the name of the Purāṇa Brahmotharakhand itself may be the name Ṛṣabha it is stated that "although you are strict follower of your duty you should avoid unnecessary killing (i.e. the necessary killing you should do; there is no harm in that)".

Śrīdharasvāmin quotes a sentence which states " the killing of a sacrificial animal enjoined by the Veda is not treated as *hiṁsā*".

The Bhāgavatapurāṇa also says "only the smelling of wine which is equal to drinking is enjoined and the touching of the sacrificial animal is enjoined by the Veda, and not killing". And Manu says "the Brahman himself created the animals for the sacrifice; the sacrifice is for the prosperity of all and therefore, the killing (of the animal) in the sacrifice is not treated as killing (i.e. *hiṁsā*)". He further says "the specific killing in this world enjoined by the Veda is to be treated as not *hiṁsā* because the Veda is the source of Dharma.

From these statements it is established that there is no sin (in killing the sacrificial animal) and therefore, there is no defect (of committing sin).

Here in the expressions *hiṁsā na hiṁsā*, *ālambhanaṁ na hiṁsā* and *vadho' vadhaḥ* unless the second words *hiṁsā* and *vadha* mean causing sin' those expressions will have no meaning.

The argument that in a killing enjoined by the veda since there is difference compared to some other killing (not enjoined by the veda), so the statement of yours is not true. Because it will not be possible to remove the similarity (of vedic killing) with the killing not enjoined by the veda. Also because of the established law that in negative sentence the direct negated is related to the absence (*abhāva*) in the relation such as being a countercorrelative delimited by the delimiting factor of correlativeness in relation to the corresponding affirmative sentence. Otherwise, in the case of non-sacrificial killing also there will arise the contingency of taking it as that (i.e. not *hiṁsā*).

Nor can you say that *na hiṁsā* means as (the sacrifice is taken) to be pure the sacrificial killing does not cause sin. Because if that is accepted then it will finally mean that the sacrificial killing causes both the desired as well as the undesired (i.e. evil) results which will lead to the contingency of its being purposeless. Because it is so known from the injunctive and prohibitive sentences. For the same season it was refuted that (in a negative sentence) the meaning of *Vidhi* is the absence of being the means of desired object.

Nor can you argue that let the statements (*hiṁsā na hiṁsā* etc.) be treated as repetitions or re-statements of the fact. Because if they are meaningful it is not possible to take them as that (i.e. as restatements). Otherwise (i.e. if such case are treated as mere restatements then) there will arise the contingency of *tatprakhyādhikaraṇa* (of Mīmāṁsā) being annulled. Therefore, it appears that the absence of sin is the expressed idea. That is why, in the Skandapurāṇa while counting the ten kinds of sin it is said "and the killing which is not enjoined (by the Veda)" and so the killing, if not enjoined by the veda, alone is said to be the producer of sin. For the same reason honourable Vyāsa formulated the *sūtra* "If you say that sacrificeial killing is not pure, it is not true. Because it is enjoined by the Veda". Therefore, since *dharmatva* and *adharmatva* are known only from the words (of Veda) and since the killing enjoined by the Veda is said to be as *dharma* that (i.e. the sacrificial killing) is not *adharma*. This is the meaning of the *sūtra* (stated above). This is how my father has explained it in his *Brahmasūtravṛtti*.

Similarly, in the statement of Manu such as "the Veda is the source of *dharma*" the being enjoined by the veda is stated as the criterion with reference to *dharma* and the intended meaning 'non-combination with *adharma* , and because of that we are to imagin a general statement having the same meaning (such as whatever is enjoined by veda is only Dharma and not *adharma*) and therefore, there is no sin in taking liquor also.

Or let there be sin in the case of taking liquor; we accept that. It is stated in the *Bhāgavatapurāṇa* etc. that since the smelling of liquor is enjoined (by the Veda) and since a little *prāyaścitta* is enjoined for that such as " (the sin caused by) telling a lie, smelling the liquor, doing sexual intercourse by day and taking the food of a *śūdra* is removed if one performs the *sandhyā* out side (his residence)", there is no harm (if taking liquor produces sin). The wise should take note of it.

Others say that by killing the animal even in the sacrifice the sin is definitely produced. The sage Vyāsa has settled this point by quoting the statement of Pañcaśikhācārya in the Pātañjalabhāṣya. The statement runs as follows:"a little sin which can be removed by little atonement rite and which can be endured is not capable of reducing the pleasure. How ? Because the pleasure is more in quantity and sin is very little (compared to the pleasure)". The meaning of this statement is this:

The construction of sentence will be the little sin caused by killing of the animal will do harm.

You cannot argue that in that case there will be no volitional effort as in the case of eating of food mixed with honey and poison. Because that (small) trouble cannot be the cause of non-inducement as the (little) labour (is not so) since it involves greater happiness. With this idea he says *svalpaḥ* etc. That (killing of a sacrificial animal) is a little (sin) is known from the statement (of Manu) therefore, killing in sacrifice is as good as not killing." Because the negative there means little as in the case of the phrase *anudarā kanyā* (the girl having a slender waist). Nor can you raise an objection taking the meaning of negative as 'absence' as in the case of *aghaṭa* (absence of pot) for this very reason there is no harm (in killing a sacrificial animal). Because when there is a possibility of application of the general prohibition (*na hiṁsyāt sarvā bhūtāni*) it is not at all possible to restrict the sphere (of that prohibition). This is why he says *supariharaḥ* i.e. which can be got rid of by performing little atonement rite. Now, even if one does not perform the rite of atonement by mistake still (the little sin) can be *sapratyavamarṣa* i.e.can be endured. Because people who are desirous of great result do endure little sorrow coming in the middle (of the entire action). Therefore, he says *kuśalasya* etc. (the opponant) asks *kasmāt*; he answers *kuśalaṁ hi* etc.

Nor can one argue that " had it been so that heaven is greater than the sin caused by the killing (of sacrificial animal) what you have said would have been true; what is the proof there? " Because we have already answered the question. Since the rite of atonement for the sin caused by the killing of (sacrificial) animal requires little wealth and effort, the sin to be destroyed by that (rite) ought to be very little; this is what can be inferred. And since a sacrifice requires lot of money and effort, the heaven produced by that (sacrifice) must be great; this is also what is inferred.

For the same reason, that even during the enjoyment of the result got through (performing) hundred *Aśvamedha*-sacrifices Indra etc. many a time get sorrows from *Rāvaṇa*, *Mahiṣāsura* etc. as stated in the *Śruti* and *Purāṇas* fits in properly. Because that the sorrow which is the result of sin caused by the killing (of the animal) in the sacrifice comes in the middle of the result of the sacrifice can be established by reason. That is why, it is stated at the end of the statement of Pañcaśikhācārya that "even in the heaven one will experience little sorrow".

Or, let the happiness and sorrow be equal(in nature). Still because of the desire of that type (i.e. desire for happiness) the volitional effort is not impossible, like the volitional effort in the case of prohibited act. Therefore, the wise people have not accepted the high state of it (the sacrifice). For the same reason it is stated in the eleventh *Skandha* of the *Bhāgavatapurāṇa* "As the smelling of liquor is enjoined by the Veda and not the drinking of it, similarly, mere touching of the animal is enjoined (in the sacrifice) and not the killing. Similarly, sexual intercourse is prescribed for the sake of progeny and not for the sake of enjoyment only. They did not understand *svadharma* this way the sacrifice is mere touching as said before and touching alone is enjoined, and not killing; rather they understood that killing alone is enjoined. This is why they do not consider this own duty (sacrifice) as *pure* because it will cause misery. For the same reason there is a *deriding* statement towards those who do not know this: "those who do not understand this, who are not good, who are *arrogant* (in their decision), who consider themselves to be honest and who are confident about their result, kill animals (in the sacrifice); when they will go to the other world after they (the animals) will eat them." This next statement (of the *Bhāgavatapurāṇa*) also, that is why, fits in.

They did not take this (killing) to be impure. *Asantaḥ* means those who are addicted to worldly enjoyment. That is why, at the conclusion (the *Bhāgavatapurāṇa*) will say (they are) away from Kṛṣṇa." *Viśrabdhāḥ* means those who are confident that by this (killing) their desire will be fulfilled. This is to be noted.

If one argues that this way (i.e. if the killing of the sacrificial animal is not done then) the sacrifice will not be performed with all its accessories (i.e. it will remain incomplete) this will be the answer : let the man get the sin. What is the difficulty in sacrifice being complete ? (i.e. one must perform the killing in sacrifice, as a consequence of it he must get the sin; the sacrifice will remain in tact. As Kumārila Bhaṭṭa has said in the *Kartradhi-karaṇa* that "If any one eats *Kalañja* etc. during the sacrifice, no defect is caused to the sacrifice because it is being performed as per the injuction (but that person alone will get the sin)".

That the *arthavādas* express the praise of what is enjoined by the *Vidhivākya* is a well-established fact and that means 'not being the cause of greater evil, Because anything other than that is inapplicable. That is why, it cannot be the meaning of *vidhi*; since (not being the cause of greater evil) is got from other source (i.e. the *arthavādavākya*) and there is no conflict between injunction and prohibition.

This is not correct. Because it has already been stated earlier that this causes greater dislike that is dispensable. Also because it is possible to explain that (the *arthavādavākyas* convey) the praise is such as 'such and such sacrifice will specifically bring quick result in a manner and so on. This is what the followers of the Sāṅkhya and the Pātañjala systems hold.

This requires re-consideration. Because it has been said that on the said statements the prohibition does not apply (to sacrifices) from that it is also not proper to postulate that sin will be less (in sacrificial killing). Because on the strength of the maxim 'there is no need of any veil for a woman who has already taken part in intercourse once' it is not possible to reduce the sin postulated on the strength of the prohibition (*na hiṁsyāt sarvā bhūtāni*) which applies without discrimination. Also because the restriction means partial annulment (i.e. you too do not accept the application in full of prohibition in the sacrificial killing).

Some say, on the same ground or reasoning that *vidhi* means three things together 1) being the means of desired object 2) being accomplishable by volitional effort and not being the cause of greater trouble than the necessary trouble required for the production of the desired object, by including in the meaning of *vidhi* not being the cause of greater trouble than the necessary trouble required for the production of desired object' also. Thus, in the case of prohibition (the negative sentence means) being the cause of evil of that type (i.e being the cause of greater trouble than necessarily required). And *vidhi* means not being the cause of that type of evil and so there is the conflict between injunction and prohibition. Therefore, the prohibition (*na hiṁsyāt sarvā bhūtāni*) does not apply to the killing enjoined by the Veda and so the killing of the animal in the Jyotiṣṭoma sacrifice is not the cause of sin. But in the case of the Vedic injunction *Śyenenābhicaran yajeta* (one should perform the Śyena-sacrifice in order to destroy the enemy) only the two such as being the means of desired object and being accomplishable by volitional effort are applied and as such there is no contradicton of the meaning of *vidhi*.

This requires here a consideration. Since the state or being necessarily required trouble cannot be defined, how that can be the meaning of *vidhi* . If you say that the state of being produced by the producer of the desired object is the definition of *nāntarīyakatva*, it is incorrect because in that case there will arise the contingency of treating hell produced by killing of brahmins and all other such prohibited acts as necessarily required. If you say that what is pervaded by the desired object is the definition of *nāntarīyakatva*, it is also not correct. Because if the *vyāpti* is time-bound then the intermediate trouble (during the sacrifice) cannot be treated as necessarily required and so the conflict with the meaning of *vidhi* . If the *vyāpti* is place-bound then there will be the defect (of contradiction between injunction and prohibition) already stated before.

If you say that being prior to the desired object is that (*nāntarīyakatva*), it is not true. Because, as it is not useful for inducing (a man in action) it cannot be the meaning of *vidhi*. And if this is taken as the inducer then there will arise the contingency of taking volitional effort with regard to a rite accomplishable by expense of huge wealth and producing very little desired object.

If it is argued that the state of not being the cause of trouble which is the object of the then greater dislike is the meaning of "not being the cause of greater trouble compared to the necessarily required trouble for the production of the desired object, it is wrong. Because not being the cause of trouble which is the object of the then greater dislike of some person is present in the case of eating of *Kalañja* also and so there will arise the contingency of absurdity of the application of the prohibition (*na kalañjaṁ bhakṣayet* one should not eat *kalañja*).

And not being the cause of (the trouble) which is the object of the dislike of all is not found in the case of *Jyotiṣṭoma* also (because some may not preform it considering the trouble in performing it) and therefore, the meaning of *vidhi* will not suit there. If you say that the state of not being the cause of a particular type of trouble is the intended meaning of that, it is incorrect. Because the trouble in performing the *Jyotiṣṭoma* may be different compared to some other trouble and so this meaning of *vidhi* does not fit in here. Not being the producer of hell is the meaning of that, if you say, it is not true. Because in the sentences one should not eat during fever, one should not do intercourse when one is affected by an eye-disease, etc. the prohibition prescribed by the Medical literature will not suit and as such the position remains the same. Although in the case of *na kalañjaṁ bhakṣayet* the negative conveys the absence of the production of hell, still in the above-mentioned cases where the result of the prohibition can be experienced (immediately) since the meaning 'not producing the hell' cannot be possible there will generate the contingency of contradiction.

In fact, although the veda conveys like that (i.e. one will go to hell if one eats *Kalañja*) still it is seen that one who does not have greater hatred (towards an act) he alone takes volitional effort and not any body else and so to postulate that sort of meaning for *vidhi* is of no use.

One cannot argue that since there will arise the contingency of sin produced by the killing of the animal in the *Jyotiṣṭoma* sacrifices etc., the pious will not take effort for *Jyotiṣṭoma* etc. and in order to avoid such difficulty 'not being the cause of greater trouble than the necessarily required trouble for the production of the desired object' is postulated as the meaning of *vidhi*. Because it has been very often stated that even though it is the cause of the trouble such as death etc. the pious do take volitional effort in performing the *Sarvasvāra-* sacrifice in which one has to offer one's self by self-immolation along with one's husband, by jumping into the *Triveṇīsaṅgama* and the like, due to extreme desire for the result (heaven).

Moreover, even if that (meaning of *vidhi*) is accepted, still the operation of the prohibition (*na hiṁsyāt sarvā bhūtāni*) cannot be restricted. Because, as in the case of *śyenenābhicaran yajeta* if the *vidhi* expresses simply the state of being the means of desired object and the state of being accormplishable by one's volitional effort on the strength of the prohibition then also operation of *vidhi* is possible. But to restrict or reduce a part of the meaning of *vidhi* with regard to the killing enjoined by the Veda is not worse in any way from the total restriction such as the non-application of the prohibition (*na hiṁsyāt sarvā bhūtāni*). The learned should think over this.

The meaning of *loṭ* is being stated by *prārthanā* (request) etc. By the word *ādi* injunction etc. and benediction are taken. Because that is understood from the *sūtras*: *āśiṣi liṅloṭau* and *loḷ ca*.

Now, the meaning of *ṅit-*(*lakāras*) is being stated in the order of *laṅ* etc.

In the sense of some action which took place yesterday and before *laṅ* is used; in the sense of inducement *liṅ*, in the sense of mere past *luṅ*; when there is the sense of non-occurrence of action (conditional) past and future *lṛṅ* is used.

Hyo bhute means the past not belonging to today. It is on the strength of the *sūtra*: *anadyatane laṅ*.

The meaning of *liṅ* is being stated by the words *preraṇādau* on the basis of the *sūtra*: *vidhinimantra-ṇāmantraṇādhīṣṭasaṁpraśnaprārthaneṣu liṅ* (p.3.3.161) (By the word *ādi* in *preraṅādau*) is included the meaning of blessing enjoined by the *sūtra*: *āśrṣi liṅloṭau* (P3.3.173).

The meaning of *luṅ* is being stated by the words *bhūtamātre* on the basis of the *sūtra* : *luṅ* (P.3.2.110) under the governing rule: *bhūte*(P3.2.84). For example *abhūt* '(some thing) happened' etc. The state of being past means being the counter corrective of the annihilative non-existence existing to-day. That applies without any difficulty to the action and so with reference to an existing pot one can say (this) pot was produced (yesterday).

The meaning of *lṛṅ* is stated by *satyām* etc. *Bhūte bhāvini* is applicable in the case of conditional (action). Thus, it means when this is the situation that one action depend on another action and when the action did not occur *lṛṅ* is to be used.

Well why do you give importance to meanings only, when other meanings of the *lakāras* are also found. If you say, the secondary signification (*lakṣaṇā*) will operate there (with reference to the other meanings) it is incorrect, because there will arise the contingency of reversion (i.e. take those other meanings as primary and those mentioned here as secondary).

Also because it will shown later that (*lakṣaṇā*) also connot apply there. If you say so, it is wrong. On the basis of the view that all words express all meanings a grammar simply declares that a particular form expressing a particular sense is correct, but it never delimits the meaning of a word. This will be stated later. Thus, with reference to some other meaning if there is some rule of grammar, the correctness of that form is nothing but desirable. What is stated in the text is mere showing the direction (i.e. giving only some examples).

If, however, the view that all word express all meanings is not accepted then one has to accept secondary signification of a word. Because that (i.e. whether a meaning is primary or secondary) can be determined on the basis of the popular acceptance frequency of the use of a word in a particular sense (i.e. the meaning frequently used will be the primary one, where as the absence of popular acceptance not frequently used will be the secondary one). But that the secondary signification stated by the Naiyāyikas, the Mīmāṁsakas and others against the grammatical rule renders the forms incorrect will be made clear by us at the proper occasion. More is going to be said in the next chapter entitled *Subarthanirṇaya.* Therefore, enough of the elaboration.

The order of the *anubandhas* alone fixes the order of these *lakāras.* This is why by saying fifth *lakāra* the Mīmāṁsakas convey *leṭ* only.

Here ends the chapter called *lakārārthanirṇaya* of the Vaiyākaraṇabhūṣaṇa.

References

1. That is to say, a past not belonging to today.
2. The text reads *dyotakatvaṁ ca śaktyādhāyakatva* which is not a happy reading and therefore we accepted the other reading given in the foot-note such as *dyotakatvaṁ ca svasamabhivyāhṛtasyaiva śaktasya bodhakatvam.*
3. Which means the special injunction *takram kauṇḍinyāya* (but the kaundinyas should be served with butter milk) sets aside the general injunction *brāhmaṇebhya dadhi diyatām* (the brahmins should be served with curd).
4. Since the definition of *vartamānatva* as *prārabdhāparisamāptatva* cannot be applicable to the actions conveyed by the verbs of the above sentences because the existence of mountains, seif is taken as eternal and as such they have no beginning.
6. That is, if *laṭ* is there *vartamānatva* is known, but if it is not there that cannot be known.
7. All the six *lakāras* ending in *t.*

8. That is.
9. That is, the *nyāya* such as a special rule sets aside the general rule does not operate in such cases.
10. That is, .if P. 3.2.123. sets aside P. 3.4.69.
11. That is, each of these types can be further divided as past and future. Thus we get *adyatana* past, *adyatana* future, *Anadyatana* past, and *anadyatana* future.
12. Here though we see the person. But we do not see him cooking. Therefore, the usage of *liṭ* perfectly grammatical.
13. The 4th *pāda* of the Introductory verse no. 3, of the *Kiraṇāvalī* on *Praśastapādabhāṣya*.
14. That is the use of *liṭ* in *vyātene* is not proper.
15. In the sentence *bahu jagāda purastāt tasya mattā kilāham.*
16. That is, the *sūtra* should have been simply *pravartanāyām liṅ.*
17. Under P. 3.3.161 : *pravartanāyaṁ liṅ ityeva suvacam. Caturṇāṁ pṛthag upādānaṁ prapañcārtham.*
18.
19. *Brahmasūtra*, 2.3.36
20. In *Vidhiviveka*, Reprint from the Pandit, p. 243.
21. The commentary one the *anuvyākhyāna.*
22. Who is without action.
23. That is, since the disk of the moon etc. can also be *iṣṭasādhana.*
24. That is, the view that *iṣṭasādhantva* is nothing but *kāryatva.*
25. Because the present *iṣṭasādhantājñāna* is definitely, there, still there is no *pravṛtti* to have the moon.
26. That is, *idānīntanatva* is an adjective of desire.
27. That is, *idānīntanatva* is an adjective of the object (result) of the desire.
28. Since it is going to be achieved after death.
29. That is, in the sense of being inducer in an act fit to be done.
30. That is, if *kāryatva* is not *vidhyartha.*
31. That is, if *iṣṭasādhanatva* is taken as the meaning of the *Vidhi.*

32. Where *buddhiviṣayatāvacchedakatva* 'being the delimiting factor of the state of being the object of knowledge or thought is the *anugamaka.*
33. That is which is the immediate cause of that thing.
34. It is a *pramāṇa* which allows the extension of significative power to convey whatever is necessary to justify the corrector of the expressed sense of which mentioned is an injunctive sentence.
36. Such as those nouns which are represented by the pronoun *tad.*
37. *Rāhūparāge snāyāt,* 'one should bathe during the eclipse (of the moon or the sun)' is the sentence that enjoins an occasional rite or *Naimittika karman* and *aharahaḥ sandhyām upāsīta* (one should perform *sandhyā* every day) is a sentence which enjoins a *nityakarman.*
38. Instead of *tva* read *sva.*
39. Because if the delimiting adjunct of *yogyatā* also becomes a primary meaning, this meaning should have some *yogyatāvacchedaka* and that *avacchedaka* will become the primary meaning which again will require *yogyatāvacchedaka* and so on and so forth. Thus endless regression.
40. To be performed in early morning, midday and evening.
41. This is in the context of the sentence : '*Audumbaro yupo bhavati*'.
42. That the injunctive sentences of *nityakarmas* do not contain any word expressive of any result and therefore *iṣṭasādhanatva* cannot be the meaning of *liṅ* and since the *vidhyartha* is not possible, no body will be induced to perform those *nityakarmas.*
43. Strictly speaking the examples should be (1) *pacanena agninā* (for *pacanaḥ agniḥ*) because though the instrumentality is expressed by the suffix *-ana,* no number is expressed by it and so instrumental case-ending cannot be avoided; (2) *Pacanyā sthālyā* (for *pacanī sthālī*) since though the location is expressed by

the suffix *-ana*, its number is not expressed and so instrumental case-ending is inevitable.

44. That is, that which is not liked by one may be liked by an other.

45. In other words, *jyotiṣṭoma*-sacrifice should be the, means to attain the heaven.

46. Because that which is invariably present immediately before the production of result can be the cause of that result. *Jyotiṣṭoma* is not such. Therefore, it cannot be the means.